KU-365-060

ROUTER TECHNIQUES
A Woodworker's Guide

Router Techniques
A WOODWORKER'S GUIDE

Kevin Harris

The Crowood Press

First published in 1994 by
The Crowood Press Ltd
Ramsbury, Marlborough
Wiltshire SN8 2HR

© Kevin Harris 1994

All rights reserved. No part of this publication may be reproduced or
transmitted in any form or by any means, electronic or mechanical,
including photography, recording, or any information storage and retrieval
system, without permission in writing from the publishers.

British Library Cataloguing-in-Publication Data
A catalogue record for this book is available from the British Library.

ISBN 1 85223 832 1

527131

MORAY DISTRICT COUNCIL

DEPARTMENT OF

LEISURE AND LIBRARIES

674.4

Picture Credits
Line-drawings by Bob Constant

Typeset by Hope Services (Abingdon) Ltd
Printed in Great Britain by The Bath Press, Avon

Contents

Acknowledgements

My sincere thanks to the people who have helped with this book, made it possible and given great encouragement along the way: to Oliver Plant, for putting my name forward for this book; my wife, Jenny, for the many hours spent at the word processor, typing up and translating my bad English into something readable; Steve Roberts, for the bulk of the excellent working photographs – he has managed to produce very good photographs despite awkward objects and situations; Andrew Platt and Nigel Harris for proof-reading and suggestions; Bill Garvey for allowing me the use of his workshop and routers at weekends.

I am grateful to the following for information about and photographs of their products, most especially Jim Phillips at Trend for information on Trend products and for photos (Jim is a highly experienced author of several router books in his own right); also (in alphabetical order) Black and Decker Ltd, Robert Bosch Ltd, Richard Huntsman of Elu, Hitachi Power Tools Ltd, Raman Weston of Leigh Industries, Luna Tools and Machinery Ltd, Des Walters of Power Rig, Martin Godfrey of WoodRat.

Introduction

The router is one of the most useful and versatile woodworking machines ever developed for the professional workshop, shopfitter, joiner, site fitter and not least the DIY enthusiast.

The range and power of the many machines available on the market means that there is one suitable for your individual needs and pocket. Only you, as an individual, can assess which make and type of router will suit you the best, but talking to other woodworkers is extremely worthwhile, as is, if at all possible, actual hands-on experience with different routers. Although it would appear on the surface to be just a machine, it soon becomes an extension of your hands and its limitations are virtually only those of its power and your imagination.

In this book, I hope to give the beginner an insight into how to use the router, along with some ideas on setting it up efficiently, as well as pass on to the professional some ideas I have had that he may not. As for myself, I too am always on the look-out for new ways to improve my use of the router. The methods I have described in this book might well suit your needs, and be helpful to you, but I hope also that other people can improve on them, or have better methods. There is always more than one way to do a job.

The technology that now supports the router is mind-blowing, from jigs and tables to the vast range of cutters that are available. If used imaginatively, the router can become a whole workshop on its own, doing all the joints, grooves, rebates and mouldings needed to make a piece of furniture, or whatever, once the timber has been prepared.

The router is not just limited to wood: with the right cutters, it can also cut plastics and soft metals, too.

The router can be used as a means of removing the bulk of waste material on a job quickly, leaving you to do the final finishing with hand tools to test your skills if that is what you enjoy; or if you are more mechanically minded, you can make and develop jigs and ways of doing the whole job with the router. Whichever way you get your kicks out of life, the router and your imagination are there to help you do the job. Enjoy your routing.

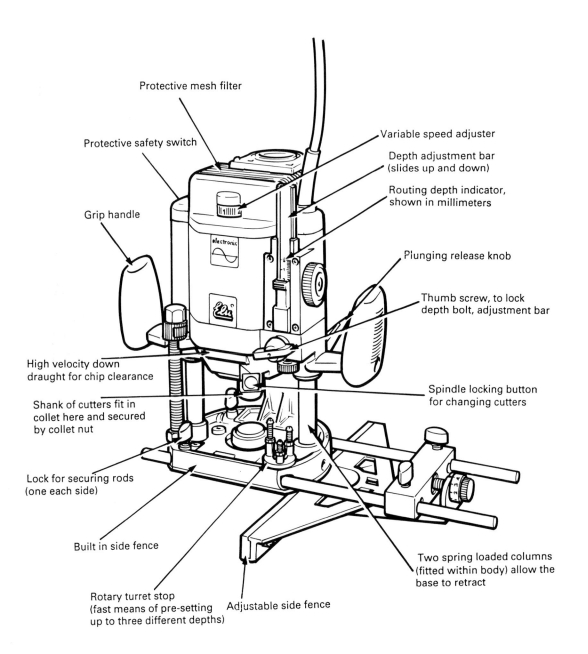

Protective mesh filter

Protective safety switch

Grip handle

Variable speed adjuster

Depth adjustment bar
(slides up and down)

Routing depth indicator,
shown in millimeters

Plunging release knob

Thumb screw, to lock
depth bolt, adjustment bar

High velocity down
draught for chip clearance

Shank of cutters fit in
collet here and secured
by collet nut

Spindle locking button
for changing cutters

Lock for securing rods
(one each side)

Built in side fence

Two spring loaded columns
(fitted within body) allow the
base to retract

Rotary turret stop
(fast means of pre-setting
up to three different depths)

Adjustable side fence

Fig 1   A typical router.

8

1 Buying a Router

At the time of writing this book there were in the region of sixteen different manufacturers supplying between them a total of sixty-three different models.

This might turn the thought of choosing a router into a nightmare, but needless to say, because of market forces and the limited amount of shelf space your local tool shop has, you can bet that you are only likely to get a choice of half a dozen of these, unless you enjoy driving around the country for the chance of buying the ultimate router, which, at this stage in life, does not exist.

The routers listed on pages 10–12 show the variation between manufacturers and, in some cases, show the different designs of basic fittings on the routers.

You, as an individual, will have to decide what router you eventually buy.

Fig 2   The Elu MOF96 Electronic with variable speed.

On some small routers the motor can be disconnected from its base and plunging mechanism. The housing where the motor fits into the base is sometimes 43mm in diameter: this is the Euro-norm, set up by European power tool companies to give a standard fitting for accessories such as drill stands.

With the motor removed, you can use the router with a rasp or burr cutters for finishing off shaping or carving.

As with all machines made and developed by different companies, each will be different in some way or another, even though ultimately they are designed to do the same job. Also, there will be a market leader for quality, and what seem to be 'good buys', as regards price.

THINGS TO CONSIDER

One of the things to consider before buying is how much you are going to use your new router. This is important for several reasons; for example, if it is for

Table 1 Router guide and specification chart.

Router Make		Model Ref No.	Watts Input	Voltage Offered		Speed Range	
				220/240	110	Fixed rpm	Variable rpm
AEG	*	OFS450S	450	√	×	27000	×
		OFS50	720	√	×	25000	×
B & D		BD66	480	√	×	26000	×
		BD780	600	√	×	30000	×
		BD780E	600	√	×	×	8–30000
BOSCH		1609K	640	√	×	30000	×
		POF400A	400	√	×	27000	×
	*	POF500A	400	√	×	27000	×
	*	POF600ACE	600	√	×	×	12–27000
		GOF900A	900	√	√	27000	×
		GOF900ACE	900	√	√	×	12–27000
		GOF1300ACE	1300	√	√	×	12–24000
		GOF1600A	1600	√	√	22000	×
		GOF1700ACE	1700	√	√	×	8–22000
ELU		MKF67	600	√	√	24000	×
		MOF96	750	√	×	24000	×
		MOF96E	900	√	√	×	8–24000
		MOF131	1300	√	√	22000	×
		MOF177	1600	√	×	20000	×
		MOF177E	1850	√	√	×	8–20000
		MOF69	600	√	×	24000	×
FESTO		OF900E	900	√	×	×	10–22000
		OF2000E	1800	√	√	×	12–22000
FREUD		FT2000E	2424	√	√	×	8–22000
HITACHI	*	FM8	550	√	√	27000	×
		M12V	1850	×	√	×	8–20000
		M12SA	1600	√	√	22000	×
		M8	800	√	√	25000	×
		M8V	800	√	√	×	10–25000
		TR6	440	√	√	30000	×
HOLZHER		2350	600	√	×	28000	×
		2355	720	√	√	25000	×
		2356	850	√	√	×	8–25000
KANGO		R8550S	850	√	√	24000	×
MAKITA		3620	860	√	×	24000	×
		3612BR	1600	√	√	23000	×
		3600B	1500	√	√	22000	×
		3700B	440	√	√	28000	×
METABO	*	OF528	500	√	√	27000	×
		OF1028	1010	√	√	27000	×
		OFE1229	1200	√	√	×	5–25500
		OF1612	1600	√	√	24000	×
		OFE1812	1800	√	√	×	8–22000
PEUGEOT		DF55E	570	√	×	×	16–2600

Router Make	Model Ref No.	Watts Input	Voltage Offered		Speed Range	
			220/240	110	Fixed rpm	Variable rpm
PORTER	100	650	×	√	22000	×
CABLE	630	745	×	√	22000	×
	690	1118	×	√	23000	×
	691	1118	×	√	23000	×
	7308–19	625	×	√	30000	×
	7518	2423	×	√	×	10–21000
	7519	2423	×	√	21000	×
	7536	1864	×	√	24000	×
	7537	1864	×	√	24000	×
	7538	2423	×	√	21000	×
	7539	2423	×	√	×	10–21000
RYOBI	R150	750	√	√	24000	×
	R500	1500	√	√	22000	×
	R600	2050	√	√	22000	×
	RE600	2050	√	√	×	10–22000
	RE120	570	√	×	×	16–26000
	TR30P	430	√	√	29000	×
SKIL	1835U	800	√	×	25000	×
	1876U1	1400	√	×	×	8–22000

*These routers have 43mm flanged collars which permit the tools to be mounted in proprietary drill stands and presses.

Router Make		Model Ref No.	Max. Plunge Depth	Collet Chuck	Net Weight (kg)
				Sizes (standard)	
AEG	*	OFS450S	50	1/4	1.8
		OFS50	50	1/4	2.5
B & D		BD66	50	1/4	2.3
		BD780	55	6mm 1/4 8mm	3.0
		BD780E	55	6mm 1/4 8mm	3.0
BOSCH		1609K	N/A	1/4	1.6
		POF400A	48	1/4	1.8
	*	POF500A	52	1/4	2.3
	*	POF600ACE	52	1/4	2.3
		GOF900A	50	1/4	3.6
		GOF900ACE	50	1/4	3.7
		GOF1300ACE	60	1/4	4.7
		GOF1600A	75	1/4 1/2	5.7
		GOF1700ACE	75	1/4 1/2	5.8
ELU		MKF67	N/A	1/4	3.3
		MOF96	55	1/4	2.8
		MOF96E	55	1/4	2.8
		MOF131	62	1/4	4.8
		MOF177	65	1/4 1/2	5.1

Router Make	Model Ref No.	Max. Plunge Depth	Collet Chuck	Net Weight (kg)
			Sizes (standard)	
	MOF177E	65	1/4 1/2	5.1
	MOF69	55	1/4	3.0
FESTO	OF900E	50	1/4	2.7
	OF2000E	65	1/4 3/8 1/2	6.2
FREUD	FT2000E	70	1/2	6.0
HITACHI *	FM8	52	1/4	2.3
	M12V	62	1/4 3/8 1/2	5.3
	M12SA	62	1/4 3/8 1/2	5.2
	M8	50	1/4	2.7
	M8V	50	1/4	2.8
	TR6	N/A	1/4	1.6
HOLZHER	2350	N/A	6mm	2.0
	2355	50	1/4	2.5
	2356	50	1/4	2.7
KANGO	R8550S	50	1/4	2.7
MAKITA	3620	35	1/4 3/8	2.4
	3612BR	65	1/4 3/8 1/2	5.7
	3600B	60	1/4 3/8 1/2	5.0
	3700B	N/A	1/4	1.6
METABO *	OF528	50	8mm	3.0
	OF1028	50	8mm	3.3
	OFE1229	50	8mm	3.4
	OF1612	60	1/2	5.0
	OFE1812	60	1/2	5.1
PEUGEOT	DF55E	55	6mm 1/4	2.4
PORTER	100	N/A	1/4	3.0
CABLE	630	N/A	1/4	3.4
	690	N/A	1/4 1/2	3.6
	691	N/A	1/4 1/2	4.2
	7308–19	N/A	1/4	2.5
	7518	N/A	1/2	6.8
	7519	N/A	1/2	6.8
	7536	N/A	1/2	6.5
	7537	N/A	1/2	6.5
	7538	76	1/2	7.8
	7539	76	1/2	7.8
RYOBI	R150	50	1/4	2.7
	R500	60	1/4	5.0
	R600	60	1/4 3/8 1/2	6.2
	RE600	60	1/4 3/8 1/2	6.2
	RE120	55	1/4	2.2
	TR30P	N/A	1/4	1.3
SKIL	1835U	50	1/4	3.2
	1876U1	63.5	1/4 1/2	4.5

*These routers have 43mm flanged collars which permit the tools to be mounted in proprietary drill stands and presses.

Fig 3   The Black and Decker BD780E.

Fig 4   The Bosch POF500A.

occasional use only, than you could get a cheap router that will not be so powerful, not such good quality and with a limited availability of attachments; but if it does the jobs that you do only once in a while, then fine. If you get a better router, it will feel better to use, will have more attachments available to buy at a later date, will probably last longer, and will have a more powerful motor. The better quality router tends to be easier to set up and to adjust, which is important if looking on a commercial basis: time is money.

As most routers are now plunging routers instead of fixed ones, it is important to try the plunging mechanism to see how well and easily it works. Plunging routers are those where the base sits on the work with the cutter up clear of the

work-piece, until you push down the handles of the machine, which pushes the cutter into the wood to the required depth. When pressure is released, the machine rises up to bring the cutter clear of the work again. The amount of plunging can be stopped and locked at any point of its travel by turning the handles or by moving a locking lever.

Are you looking for a router to do a specific job, which it will always be set up for, such as running mouldings? If so, you not only have to consider the router itself, but whether it would be beneficial to buy a purpose-made router table, in which you could turn the router upside down to form a small spindle moulder. In that case you should look at the many router tables on the market, or could

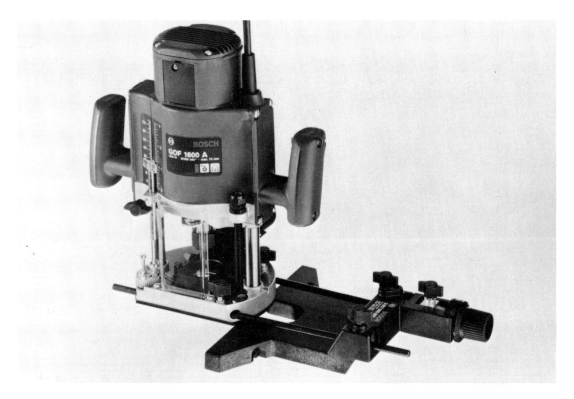

Fig 5   The Bosch GOF1600A.

make your own table, as a keen and imaginative woodworker!

In certain cases, where you have a specific job in mind, you may find that you have to start in reverse order, in that the cutter you need to do the job may only be made with a ½in (12mm) shank (because of the cutter size), which would stipulate that you have to buy a router capable of taking a ½in (12mm) shank cutter. Once you have got over the shock of having to buy a bigger router than you had intended, you will appreciate the advantage of being able to use any shank-size cutter in the future. Collet reducers (which enable you to do this) may come with your router, or may be bought as an extra, to take ⅜in (8mm) and ¼in (6mm) shank cutters.

Size and Weight

Another thing to consider is the size and weight of the router, which of course goes along with power; you may decide that the bigger, more powerful router seems a good idea, but is it? If you will only be doing small intricate work, trying to keep under control a router that could be as much as 4½lb (2kg) heavier than you need for the job you are doing, seems like unnecessarily hard work to me. For the sake of the odd time when you might need to make very big rebates or grooves (which you can do with a small router, only with more stages and slower feed speed), is it worth the other 90 per cent of times spent struggling with an over-sized powerful router?

14

Fixed-Speed or Variable Speed

Yet another factor to take into consideration is whether to have one at fixed speed or with electronically variable speeds. Fixed-speed routers give you one speed, dependent on the make of the machine, usually running at about 20–24,000 rpm. Variable-speed routers allow you, by turning a knob on the machine, to reduce or increase the speed of the motor in the range of 8,000 to 27,000 rpm, depending on the make of router. The electronic-speed router has several advantages over fixed-speed routers, one being that when you start the router, it does not kick into life, but starts very gently; this is known as soft start, and is especially noticeable on the big routers. Be warned that, with big fixed-speed routers, the kick from starting is quite impressive; always hold on to it with both hands!

The noise level is much lower on the variable-speed routers, especially at low speeds, which, in turn, makes the router less tiring to use and gives you more control. The variable speed option also gives you a great advantage in improving the quality of finish a cutter produces on certain timbers, for example by preventing burning on end-grain mouldings.

Switches

It is important for the router to have an easily operated on/off switch that you can locate and use without necessarily knowing where to look for it. If you do not have a friend who has a router and can give you a try and, hopefully, some basic instruction on his machine, then go along to a good tool shop where you may be given good advice and information about practical courses.

Fig 6   The Hitachi M8V.

Fig 7   The Ryobi RE120.

Grip

Choose a model that suits you – do not be shy in the shop, try them all and see if they feel right to you, even if you hold them upside-down.

Voltage

When buying a router it is most important to decide whether or not you want a 110-volt or a 240-volt one. The advantages of 110-volt motors are that they wear better, and are safer (*see also* page 118).

Always read the manufacturer's instruction manuals before using the machine, and a book or two. If you have to teach yourself, then please make sure someone knows that you are using an electrical machine with which you are not familiar, so that they can keep a discreet eye on you, or go to an evening class, for example.

Fig 8   The Bosch 1604 router, non-plunging type. The depth of cut is determined by the rotation of the motor inside the base. This type of router has been superseded by the plunging type.

2 Accessories and Attachments

Accessories and attachments include things like extra collets, guide bushes, guide-bush holders, fine fence and fine height adjusters, trammel bars and bases, edge followers and guides, base-plate extensions, sub-bases, tracking set and guide-rails. Also available are router tables, and racks that hold the router upside-down or on its side, overhead or

Fig 10   The Elu 40900 moulding kit.

even at an angle if you wish. These tables and racks then have their own sets of attachments and accessories that you might need; or can you make your own? The possibilities are endless.

There are bench-mounted tables and floor-standing tables. When looking at tables, you must consider what you hope to do on them, as this will help you to work out which will be most suitable for you. The strength of the table is important, as the weight and leverage to which you can subject a table with a long or heavy piece of wood is quite extreme. Small, bench-mounted tables need to be

Fig 9   The Elu 551 table.

Fig 11   The Luna Universal router stand.

Fig 12   The SI-2 saw/router bench from Luna Tools.

secured to the bench on a flat area so that the table does not tip over or get twisted and distorted; if this happens, working accurately becomes very awkward.

With floor-mounted tables, it is important to make sure that they are stable and do not slide about on a smooth surface, and that the weight of timber you are putting on them is not too much for the table. These tables are a wonderful investment if you have the use for them; however, good equipment costs money.

A home-made table may suit your pocket and needs perfectly adequately, especially if you have the time to spend designing and making a table yourself. Your own skills and perhaps other practical interests may give you ideas on what you can make your own table out of; for example, metal or plastic. If you think about it, what does a table do? It holds the router upside-down, so you need to consider how to hold it; the fence rods are an easy way, so can you design your table to use these?

The table needs a flat surface, such as a man-made board with a piece of plastic laminate glued on top, which will give a nice smooth surface to run your wood over. Rout a hole in it, for the router cutter to project through, then some sort of fence to keep the work-piece in line with the cutter. This can be as simple as a straight edge with two cramps to hold the fence in place, or you can make a more sophisticated one with some slots in the table surface and a couple of bolts with wing nuts, which are easier to adjust and mean you do not have to put up with cramps getting in the way. Now make a stand or frame to fix this to, and devise some method of holding it to your bench, and – wow! – another useful piece of equipment emerges out of workshop scraps! There are plenty of publications available showing how to make a table for yourself.

ROUTER ATTACHMENTS

Most routers come with basic attachments like fences, and nowadays with dust-extraction hoods as well. Some firms make up accessory kits to do certain jobs. As with the router itself, you are the one to decide what attachments you will need. One of the best ways to approach this situation is to wait until you have a need for a particular attachment, and then assess which one is best for you. Some attachments sound a great idea, especially if you are talking to a good sales rep who is on commission. Some things, like fine fence and height adjusters, do make fine adjustment easier, but I would not say they are essential. Quite often these need to be bought for use with some other accessory; usually, in this case, the manufacturer's catalogue points out all the parts you need, or suggests which bits will be needed to use the jig successfully.

I find a second fence useful because I remove the plastic guides and put a continuous piece of wood on them, one the size of the fence itself and one slightly longer and wider. This helps to keep the router more stable and reduces the chance of rolling the router around the end of your work-piece.

Guide Bushes

These are fixed to the base of the router, usually by two machine screws. The guide bush guides the router along a specific path with the guide bush in contact with the jig. Some manufacturers supply a bush with the router. If not, you can purchase them: Elu, for instance, offer a range of bushes from 10mm to 30mm outer diameter, for their machines.

Fig 13   Leigh Industries Universal set of guide bushes.

Leigh Industries have developed a universal set of guide bushes to use with most makes of router. This may be useful if your particular make of router has only a limited range of guide bushes, or if you want to use different makes of router with the same jig.

> The outer diameter of the bush affects your jig, and the inner diameter restricts cutter diameter, but remember that the outer bush diameter and the cutter diameter need to be considered together when making jigs for specific jobs.

Fig 14   A router fitted with a fine height adjuster, which replaces the standard depth stop as seen at the side of the router.

Fine Height Adjuster

This is usually in the form of a rod with a hollow threaded section at the bottom end, which screws on to a threaded bolt on the turret stop (depth stops), and a knob at the other end with which to turn the bar.

With some makes and models of router it is an extra piece of equipment, while on others it is built into the router itself. It is designed for very fine setting of the depth of cut, and it also turns your router into a fixed router. You need this with some attachments, or if you are going to use the router upside-down as a spindle moulder.

Fine Fence Adjuster

This is a threaded rod, with either a fixed or a separate knob; one end is screwed into the router base, and the knob is attached to the fence. You then simply turn the knob to move the fence in or away from the cutter to give accurate final adjustment. Some manufacturers make a fence with a micro-adjustment built into it; in most cases the fine adjustment is only over a small distance, but is still sufficient.

Trammel Bars and Bases

These are for cutting whole circles and

20

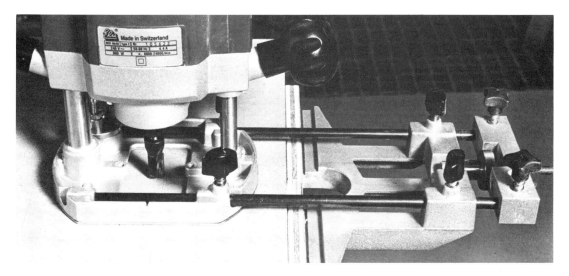

Fig 15 A router fitted with a side fence, which is itself fitted with a fine fence adjuster.

parts of circles on flat materials. There are sub-bases with pins in, which can be positioned within the base sizes of the router for small radii. Then for radii of up to about 15in (380mm), trammel bars are used. These consist of steel bars that attach to the fence-rod fixing points on the base of the router; at the other end there is an adjustable pin to pivot the router around, with a hand knob on top to hold it in position. Then there is the home-made trammel bar, which can be a length of ply or other suitable board, with a hole near one end the size of a guide bush, in which to locate the router; a nail or screw is used as the pivot point at the required distance along the bar.

ROUTER ACCESSORIES

Radial-Arm Saw

This is a circular saw that pulls out over a table to cut timber to size. This machine can also be used to mount a router on, giving you an overhead router, which you can fix to be static, or you can use the radial-arm mechanism to move the router on a defined path. This can be at 90 degrees to the fence, or at any angle within the 90-degree swing of the arm of the machine, making the repetition of, say, angled slots across a board, safe and accurate. By leaving the machine unlocked, to be swung, you can use it to guide the router in an arc of any size within the distance of travel the arm allows. When using the router this way, you must clamp your work down on the table safely.

These machines have the capacity to tilt the blade from 90 degrees to 45 degrees to the table of the machine. I am sure you could put this to good use, for example to make angled grooves and rebates, using a straight cutter. I would not suggest that you go straight out and buy a radial-arm saw; if you have one, however, can you use it as an overhead router?

To mount the router on to the radial-arm saw, you either have to make a bracket yourself, or purchase a ready-made one.

Fig 16   A radial-arm saw.

Dovetail Jigs

Leigh Dovetail Jig

This is a well-made and well-developed jig, which will guide the router in such a way that you can make through, half-blind, sliding and end-to-end dovetails. Also, with this jig, you can make dovetails at angles other than 90 degrees; to do this, you use packers in the clamping bars, and prepare the ends of your boards by cutting to the desired angle across the width of the board. In this way, it is possible to produce compound angles. The jig works by having adjustable finger bars, which guide the router. The router is fitted with the appropriate size guide bush. The finger bars are individually adjustable to give you the size and spacing of the dovetails you would like.

Once you have set the finger bars, either for the tails or pins, the other is automatically set, that is, if you adjust the finger bars for the tail setting you want, the appropriate pin setting is automatically selected, and vice versa. Because you can space the joints out to the distance you need, up to a width of 24in (600mm) for the bigger jig, you do not get the problem of odd-sized pins and tails at each end of a row of joints, as you do with some dovetail jigs.

This jig is ideal for batch production, or for someone who likes to have decoratively spaced dovetails of different patterns. The tails are cut using specific-degree dovetail cutters, and straight

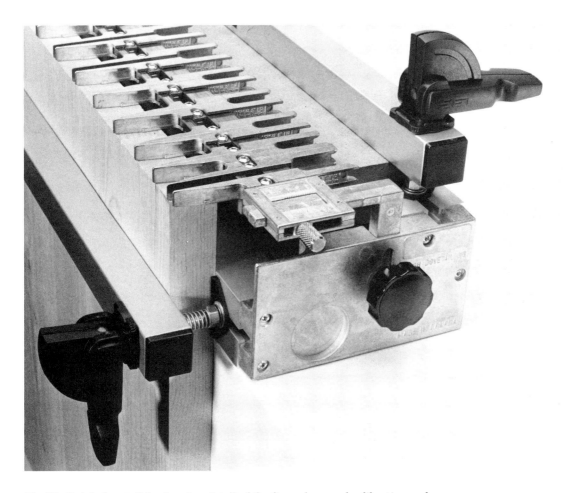

Fig 17   Leigh dovetail jig showing detail of the finger bars and calibration scale.

cutters for the pins, so unless you possess two routers, you have to change cutters at some point. It is recommended that you use a router of at least 1hp (900 watts) or above. The accuracy of the fit of the joint is ensured by micro-adjustment on the jig, and the use of the fine depth adjuster on the router itself.

A comprehensive manual comes with the jig, and a video is also available, which goes through the operations very clearly. I would suggest that it is worth buying the video; and if at all possible, I would recommend that you be shown how to work the jig in person.

Elu Dovetail Jig, Models A and B

Model A is for use with MOF96 routers and model B is for use with MOF131 and 177(E) routers. With model B, an adaptor sub-base is supplied as standard. Small modifications are needed to make bases fit on to other makes of router, which have to have one dimension of their bases less than 6in (150mm).

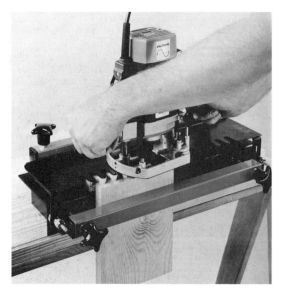

Fig 18   Elu dovetail jig.

The maximum working width is 12in (300mm), and the board can be ½-1¼in (13–32mm) thick. As you can see in fig 18, the jig sits on the bench at the front edge to allow for the front board to be clamped in vertically. The jig needs to be screwed, or clamped, to the bench. Furthermore, a fine vertical adjuster is recommended for use with this jig, to make accurate setting easier.

Elu Multifunctional Dovetail Jig

This is a bigger and more sophisticated jig: not only can it produce a run of dovetails up to 24in (610mm), but it can produce comb joints and dowel joints using extra optional templates. Three different

Fig 19   Elu multifunctional dovetail jig.

sizes of dovetail pitch can be produced by using optional dovetail templates, as well. Adjustable stops are fitted, so that you can equalize the joints at each end.

This jig works like other dovetail jigs: the router is guided around the template with a certain size guide bush fitted to the router base. Also, dovetail cutters of a certain size and angle need to be used with the correct template. Trend make the correct cutters for the Elu Multi-functional, and the reference numbers are given with the instructions. As with most dovetail jigs of this kind, both parts of the joint are cut at the same time. The big drawback is the fixed size of the dovetail, which means careful consideration has to be given to what happens at each end of the joints, otherwise you could end up with odd-sized parts of a joint.

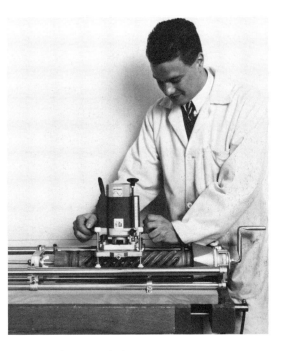

Fig 20   The Routerlathe.

Routerlathe

The Routerlathe makes use of the portable router to shape or decorate turned section timber, such as table legs. It is basically four bars, which hold a headstock and tailstock apart, in between which the wood to be shaped is held. The headstock has a cranked handle, which is used to rotate the wood, and an index pin and cable winding, which pulls the router along in time with the rotation of the work-piece.

The router is mounted on a base, which is located on the back top bar. On the base are two level adjuster screws, and a template follower pin, which runs along the template held vertically in front of the lathe if copy turning is done.

Work that can be carried out on the lathe includes:

1   Straight beads and flutes cut parallel to the work-piece, along its length, straight or tapered.
2   Spiralling or roping, right and left hand at 45 degrees.
3   Beads and coves around the work-piece, achieved by using different shaped cutters.
4   Shaped turning by using a template to follow a shape that you have cut out.

With the vast range of cutters available of all shapes and sizes, it gives you the chance to design your own patterns and shapes and to produce some unusual turned shapes.

Routerack, by Trend

The Routerack is a set of components that can be purchased separately, or as sets, to

25

Figs 21(a–e)   The Routerack by Trend.

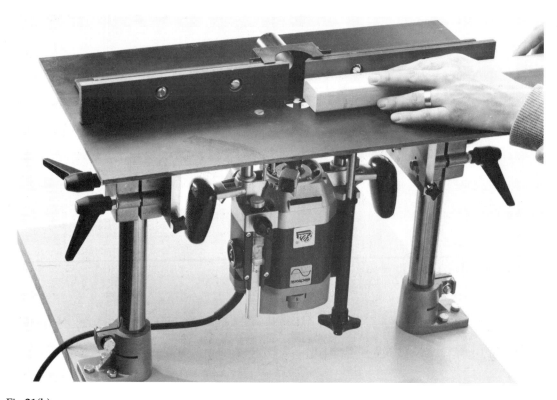

Fig 21(b).

turn your router into a multi-use machine. The uses to which you can put this rack are possibly limited only by the size of your work-piece. As you can see in figs 21(a–e), the rack can hold a router in every position that a router ever needs to be held in. Fig 21(a) shows the router being held horizontally in the Routerack; the two fences that are set at 90 degrees to each other have been removed to show how the router is held. In this position, it can be used as a slot mortiser. In fig 21(b), the router is inverted and is being used as a small spindle moulder. Of course the fence can be removed to leave you with a router table. In fig 21(c) the router is in use as a fixed overhead router, and in fig 21(d) as an overhead milling machine; in con-

Fig 21(c).

Fig 21(d).

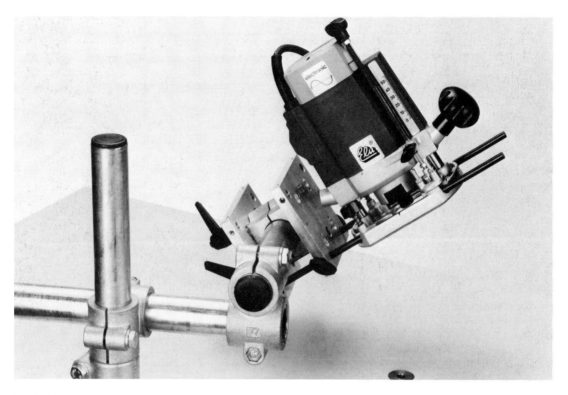

Fig 21(e).

junction with a compound machine table, the latter set-up would be ideal for small, accurate components. Because of the use of round tubes and 90-degree brackets, which clamp the tubes together, you can set your router at whatever angle you need to carry out the desired operation, as shown in fig 21(e).

Routergraph Sign Router

The Trend Routergraph uses a pantograph of 1:1 fixed ratio and is designed to be used with the small MOF96 router; it can take other makes of small routers, however. It works by guiding the stylus in either a ready-made letter template, of which several styles are available, or whole sentences of standard signs; they come in plastic, or sets of brass templates. Alternatively, you may wish to make your own templates. The Routergraph can be purchased as a basic pantograph, for which you need to make up a table and clamping devices, or these can be bought as extras. Other extras include a circle-cutting device, different sized styli, and a sliding base and pillar to extend the machine to take longer signs or shapes.

Ellipse- and Circle-Cutting Jig

This jig was designed by a furniture manufacturer and is produced and sold by Trend. It allows you to cut ellipses very accurately and simply, by means of two

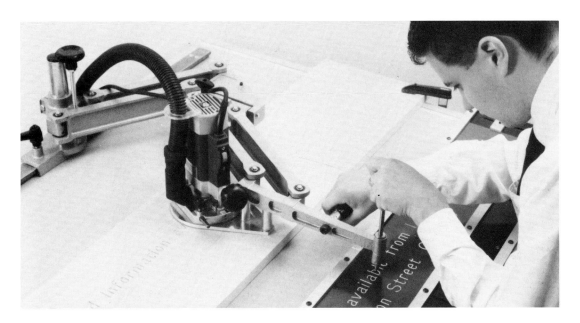

Fig 22 The Routergraph sign router.

Fig 23 Ellipse- and circle-cutting jig.

Major Axis (in/mm)	Minor Axis (in/mm)	
	Max	Min
70¾/1,800	65/1,650	55/1,400
59/1,500	53/1,350	43¼/1,400
48/1,200	41¼/1,050	31½/800
36/900	30/760	21¾/550
31½/800	25½/650	21¾/550
27½/700	21¾/550	21¾/550

Table 2 Largest and smallest possible sizes for ellipses, using an ellipse- and circle-cutting jig.

sliding pivot points which slide in dovetail slots at 90 degrees to each other.

The bar that runs through the pivot points is attached to a connector plate, which fits directly on to the fence rods of Elu routers. Other makes of router can be attached by the use of a false base plate fitted to the bar adaptor. By using only one slide the jig can be used to cut circles. Table 2 shows the limitations on the sizes of the ellipses that can be cut.

Mini Ellipse- and Circle-Cutting Jig

This is a smaller version of the larger ellipse jig, designed to produce smaller ellipses using small routers which fit on to the plastic plate, which is also the integral bar to which the two pivot points are attached.

A plotter pen and plug is supplied with the jig, which will then turn the jig into a drawing instrument for ellipses or, as with its big brother, by removing one of the slides and using a special pin, the jig can then be used to cut circles up to 12in (30cm) in diameter.

Table 3 shows the limitations of sizes of ellipses that can be cut from the mini ellipse.

The WoodRat

The following account has very kindly been supplied by the WoodRat's inventor, Martin Godfrey.

Developed by Martin Godfrey, in Britain, this joint-cutting mill is designed and precision engineered to a high standard. Its means of cutting is a

Major Axis (in/mm)	Minor Axis (in/mm)	
	Max	Min
22¾/580	20½/520	17/430
19⅝/500	18/450	14/360
15¾/400	13⅜/340	9⅞/250
12/300	9⅞/250	6¼/160
8⅝/220	6¼/160	6¼/160

Table 3 Largest and smallest possible sizes for ellipses, using a mini ellipse jig.

Fig 24   Mini ellipse- and circle-cutting jig.

Fig 25   The WoodRat joint-cutting mill.

plunge router: any make can be used. The way in which the router is held in the machine, guided by a series of sliding plates and cams, allows you to make straight or angled cuts to a high degree of accuracy. The cutter is thus moved through the wood, but the router itself can be fixed, and the timber moved, horizontally left or right, so that the wood is moved through the cutter. Tenons can be cut in four simply set movements of router and bar. Laps and tongues or raised and fielded panels are made with one or two settings.

The wood is tracked by a wheel positioned on the top of the machine, which operates a sliding bar by means of a wire and pulley drive (the bar slides are replaceable phenolic runners). On this bar, the timber is held, in most cases by the edges, by means of quick-release cam clamps.

Timber can also be hand-fed under the router against the face of the machine and up under the plate like an inverted router table, for profiling and trenching, and cutting grooves for lids and drawer bottoms.

When cutting dovetails, dovetail jigs require metal templates or some kind of fixed or movable fingers to guide the router. The WoodRat has no need of these. Instead, there are two positions on the sliding bar to lock the two pieces to be joined. On the left, one piece is simply marked with pencil marks where the joints are to be (the parallelogram gives even spacing). These pencil marks are tracked in turn against a mark drawn on a paper label which is the size and shape of the cutter in use. While at each position, on the right-hand side, the corresponding board is cut by a dovetail cutter. When all the drawer sides, or box sides, are dovetailed, they are themselves used on the left as templates. The dovetail cutter is changed for a straight cutter and the

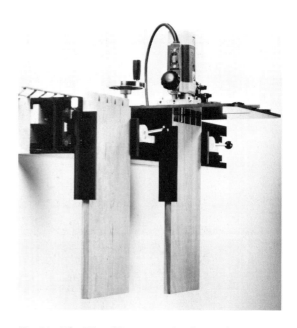

Fig 26   The WoodRat set up for dovetailing.

sliding plates are rearranged to cut the pins. This way the machine will cut all kinds of dovetail – through, half-blind, cogged, mitred or double-lapped – with any spacing. WoodRat supply a range of eight high-speed steel cutters developed for use with the machine, from 4mm up to a massive 50mm deep. The WoodRat will also dovetail boards from 20mm to 750mm wide.

The machine is capable of cutting all the joints needed to make furniture. Due to the way the machine controls the router, it is possible to run the wood into the cutter on the back-cut or down-cut, since the wood is, as it were, power-fed. This will do away with break-out, which is a constant problem when cutting across the grain. For a machine capable of so many operations, it does not need a lot of space, being best hung on any sturdy wall with about 2 metres of clear space available. It can be bench mounted, but you will really need your bench to work with the machine.

Fig 27   The Power Rig.

The main body of the machine is a large aluminium extrusion. This can be fitted to an extractor to remove the waste directly from the cutter area. When the cutter is not actually cutting it is parked safely in the body of the machine out of harm's way. As the router is not used free, one can expect a longer life for both router bearings and for cutters.

The Power Rig

This was invented by Des Walters and is made from aluminium extrusion and rigid plastic. This table is designed to hold power tools above the work-piece, with you controlling the tools; or else the table can be used to hold the tools upside-down with the cutters protruding upwards, you handling the work-piece. Two sizes are available to choose from. The table is light and simple to assemble, which makes it ideal for someone with limited space to work in, or who has to put the table away each time after use; or it can be used for site work, being easy to transport from site to site. The Power Rig can either be bench-mounted, or, as an extra, a slot-together tubular steel stand, with a third leg to support long material, is available.

3 Safety and Set-Up

A major factor to consider is personal safety, so we'll start with that – this includes ear-defenders, ear-plugs, eye protection in the form of goggles, safety glasses, full-face visors or face helmets, as well as dust-extraction, cabling, cutter safety, working conditions, and so on.

PERSONAL SAFETY

Ear-Defenders

These are needed because of the high-pitched whine of the router. If you are using your router for long periods of time, it can cause you to lose concentration, which isn't good for you – you could trim your fingernails a bit more closely than you might like! You could also make mistakes in your work, apart from possibly damaging your ears.

You can get varying quality ear-defenders, and it's worth buying good ones, that are suitable for using with high-pitched noise machinery. If you find that ear-muffs are unsuitable or unsatisfactory for you, then ear-plugs could be a possibility. It's up to you to find what is most suitable for you to use.

Because of noise problems when sharing premises, some workshops have separate rooms, or booths, for router work.

Eye Protection

Safety glasses are cheap, reasonably com-

fortable to wear, and don't usually get in the way too much. One problem that does occur quite a bit is that chips of wood manage to bounce up off your face and go underneath the glasses. Face visors are worthwhile to protect other parts of your face or your mouth. They are reasonably comfortable to wear and you can flip them up out of the way very easily when not needed.

Breathing Apparatus

A piece of cheap, disposable equipment is the dust-mask, which covers your mouth and nose. There are varying qualities on the market; again, it will be up to you to find which is most comfortable and most suitable for you, and at a price you are willing to pay. It is worth remembering, though, that it is not just the dust that can cause you harm; there is often harmful chemical glue in man-made board, which may have toxic and carcinogenic properties. So always buy a good, industry-approved mask.

One piece of safety equipment that is extremely useful, especially to the commercial business or workshop that uses a router or dusty materials a lot, is a full-face helmet, or visor, with an in-built filter system. There are several on the market that do the job extremely well. They filter the air, usually via a back-pack, which you strap on; air travels through a tube up into the head-piece and down over your face. This also pre-

Fig 28   Personal safety equipment.

vents the visor from misting up, while giving you clean, fresh air to breathe. There are others that have the motor and the filter in the head-piece, so that there is no back-pack, or pipes running down your back. These are extremely good in that they give you clean, filtered air, so that you don't need to worry about dust extraction going directly to the machine, which can, in some circumstances, be awkward because it is another tube to control and to keep out of the way. These visors, or head-pieces, usually run on rechargeable batteries and are very expensive to buy, but if you are using a router a lot, they are worth the cost for your own peace of mind and safety.

With all this safety gear on, you often feel more like a spaceman than a wood-worker! However, you will soon become used to it and will find ways of making it easier to bear.

TOOL SAFETY

Cables and Dust-Extraction Pipes

Cables fixed to the router are a safety problem. It is always hard to keep them in the best position for working and out of the way. The main power cable to the router needs to be managed, too, so that it doesn't get tied up with cramps or get caught on pieces of wood and projecting jigs. You can be pulling the router along one moment, and then find that it has stopped for no apparent reason; it is usu-ally because the cable has become tied up around a G-cramp, or caught under a jig. Also be very careful when putting the machine down, so that you don't place it on the cable and cut it; this is especially easy to do if you have the router locked in plunged mode with the cutter project-ing through the base. Plunging routers are normally a lot safer, as the base pro-trudes beyond the cutter when it is released from its plunging action. With the cutter safely up above the base you can put the router down directly on to the bench without worrying. However, don't let go of the machine until the motor has stopped rotating.

Dust-extraction pipes to the router, particularly of large diameter, can cause problems. If you are working in a bench situation, and can suspend the lead and the dust-pipe from the ceiling, so that it is directly above you rather than dragging across the bench, then you will be able to

35

Fig 29 Elu dust-extractors are wired up to connect power tools to the units, which then start the extractor as you switch on the power tool.

keep it out of harm's way. If this is not possible, an alternative method of keeping the cable and dust-extraction pipe out of the way is to actually have them slung over your shoulder so that they follow along with you, rather than having them in front of you. This is both safer and quick to set up.

Elu makes three types of dust extractor; in each case, you plug your portable tool into a socket on the extractor, which is wired up so that it starts and stops when you start and stop your router, or whatever tool you may be using, so that you don't need to remember to switch on the extractor beforehand.

Cutters

Safety as regards the cutter in the router machine itself must always be taken seriously. The cutter is dangerous all the time it is rotating, so if you want to make any adjustments on the machine, such as alter any settings, it is important to stop the machine and let it come to rest before actually making the alterations. When changing the cutter itself, it is advisable to switch off the power at the socket, or to unplug the router.

The cutter must always be clamped into its collet correctly and safely: read the instruction manual for your particular machine. Over-stressing the machine or the cutter by cutting too deeply or too fast can cause the cutter to vibrate and, in some cases, can loosen the collets and eventually the cutter, which may either drop out or fly out. At any sign of undue vibration or noise, stop the machine and check to see that the collet is tight, and also that the fence mechanisms are not coming loose. Always be aware of any unfamiliar noises.

Always hold the router with both hands when starting it: be aware of the fact that, as with most machines, it will kick when first started. On variable-speed machines with the soft start there is less of a problem, but it is still worth holding on to the machine with two hands when starting, to be on the safe side. Make sure you know where the on/off switch is, and how easily and effectively you can switch it on and off, before you actually use the router.

Another safety consideration, as far as holding the machine is concerned, is to make sure that when you use the plunging mechanism, you apply pressure evenly on both sides of the machine when pressing down. If too much pressure is put on one side, you will sometimes find that it will just stick, so that it won't plunge smoothly. Another reason for this problem could be that the plunging shafts need cleaning.

Router Cutters below 5mm in Diameter

These are extremely easy to break if they are forced too fast through a piece of wood. When you get down to 2mm or 1.6mm, the smallest that you can get, they will break for a pastime if you are not extremely cautious when feeding them through the timber. You should be very wary, especially if you are using them to make deep cuts; it really is worth taking a bit more time and care, rather than breaking the cutter and possibly injuring yourself in the process.

Big Router Cutters

One of the danger factors with these is actually the power (the kick) that they can create if, for some reason, you actually start the machine up with the cutter already touching the wood. You don't necessarily break the cutter, but it could certainly make a nasty mess of the work you are doing, or, at the very least, throw the whole machine about! Before starting up, therefore, make sure that the cutter is well clear of the material that you are about to cut, and that you are feeding it the right way.

Changing Router Cutters

First, **switch the machine off at the mains!** Also when changing router cut-

ters, be aware that if you've just used a router cutter before changing it over, you might find that it is too hot when you go to handle it. They do get extremely hot, so be very cautious.

THE WORKING AREA

As you will be concentrating on your machining and what you are actually doing, it is certainly advisable to have the area around your feet, where you are going to be walking to and fro while you are using the router, safely clear of tools, wood or any other obstacle. One of the dangers that does build up without notice is dust. The very fine dust produced from routing will, on certain floors, be amazingly slippery. One in particular is the dust from MDF (medium-density fibreboard), which is extremely dangerous, as it becomes very slippery when there is a build-up after a bit of time spent routing. Be extremely wary of this.

Dummy Runs with the Router

It is sometimes worth doing a dummy run, without actually running the machine. Just slide the router along your projected line of cut to make sure that it, or your jig attachment, doesn't run into something that you haven't noticed, get tangled up in your cable, or come across some other obstacle that you hadn't been aware of previously. If you find you have a clear run, then, hopefully, it is safe to proceed with your cut.

Site Work

When carrying out site work there are

other dangers to consider, for if you are altering or modifying work that is already in place and in use, metal fixings such as screws and nails may be in your line of cut. A good inspection is always worthwhile. A tungsten cutter will go through soft steel or brass screws, but the router will kick back. When using the router to cut access panels and holes, consider what may be behind them – water pipes, electric cables, or similar hazards. Protect yourself!

Here concentration is all important, for there are usually many other people working. This means much more noise, sometimes when you least expect it, and many more interruptions. It's much easier to damage finished work than when working on your own – and for your new router to 'walk' when your back is turned.

> On big building sites the use of only 110-volt machinery is permitted. 110 volts will not kill you, but 240 volts can.

SAFETY WHILE ROUTING

Holding Down and Cramping

Holding down and cramping your work is an extremely important safety factor. If it is not securely held, or fixed down on to the bench, it could come loose and, if it is a small piece of wood, fly up and hit you. When using big routers with big cutters, the vibration can be quite severe, and in some cases pieces of wood do come loose, quite easily, from their cramped position. Experience will tell

Fig 30   Selection of cramps (you always need them in pairs).

you how much force to use, and how best to cramp things down; experience will also help you to recognize, from the noise and vibration emitted by the router, how much strain you are putting on the wood. Always be conscious of how much pressure you are putting on your work-piece.

As you can see from Chapter 2, there is an array of purpose-made tables and jigs available to hold your work when using the router. One of these may well suit your needs perfectly. For myself, the woodworkers' work-bench is my main means of cramping work to be routed. If the work-piece is too big for the bench, then it goes on to a pair of trestles; if the pieces are too small to be held on my

Fig 31 The router mat being used while trimming laminated board.

bench, then I mount an Elu E40900 moulding table on my bench, and feed the work-pieces over this table. However, recently I have started to use a 'router mat'. This is a rubberized mat which grips the work-piece and the bench surface when even slight downward pressure is put on the work-piece.

With this mat there is no need to cramp down your work-piece; and if there are no cramps in the way of your working, you can make a continuous run all the way around the board in one go, as shown in fig 31, where a laminated board is being trimmed up. As this mat is

still a new method of holding work, I cannot say at this time how much of a cut can be taken, or how much gripping power the mat has before the piece moves. It hardly needs to be pointed out that the surfaces of your bench and work-piece need to be clean and flat to get full grip from the mat. I have been informed that certain types of carpet underlay will work as well. The size of the mat I have been using is about 3ft (90cm) long, 2ft (60cm) wide and ¼in (6mm) thick.

Holding objects that cannot be held in or on the bench, or out on site, does create its own set of problems. The good old

Fig 32   Here wood blocks are used to hold
a door on its edge safely, while hinge
recesses are being routed.

Routing on a Table

If you are using the router upside-down in a table, or in a manner similar to a spindle-moulding situation where your cutter is protruding up through the base, the main problem is that you are usually feeding very small pieces of wood past the cutter, which means that your fingers are very vulnerable. If you can get into a situation whereby you can use the pressure pads in both directions to push your wood in against the fences, so that the cutter is totally enclosed, this is ideal. However, in many circumstances this simply cannot be done, especially if you are using a ball-bearing guide over the top of the cutter to run the jig around, or if you are forming some sort of moulding, or rebate, on the underside of the wood. In these cases, you will just have to be extremely cautious and careful where you position your fingers on your piece of wood.

Bench-mounted tables must be fixed down securely and, especially during long periods of use, it is worthwhile checking these fixings every so often. When mounting the router in the table, make sure you have positioned the router with the on/off switch to the front, facing you; it is obviously not a good idea to put your hand in under the table, and poke around, trying to find the switch in a hurry.

For your own health, to avoid back pain, set the table on a bench at a height that makes using the router comfortable. Floor-mounted tables should be set up so that they are stable and sit firmly, and do not slide across the floor when you push the work across the table; it might be necessary to anchor the feet to the floor in some way to stop this.

Black and Decker WorkMate is probably the best known, and most used, device in these situations. Do not forget to refer to Chapter 2 for other ideas for suitable tables and rigs. Another method I have used to hold doors and table-tops on edge, is to use two blocks of wood with a housing cut out to receive the edge of the door, together with a large wedge, which holds the door vertically, as in fig 32. These are easy to make and use.

Whatever you use to hold or cramp your work, it must be strong enough for you to proceed safely and efficiently.

Other Unforeseen Dangers

Be warned that there may be particles coming out of the wood that are not necessarily timber. In chipboard, in particular, there are quite often foreign bodies such as bits of stone or metal, which are not seen, or not noticed – if one of these hits you, you will know about it! Routing man-made boards, especially chipboard, also seems to destroy router cutters at an amazing rate. If you look at your router cutter closely, especially if it is tipped with tungsten, you might see that you have lost the odd bit of cutter. These pieces must have flown off somewhere – hopefully they haven't gone into your face!

GENERAL SAFETY OF ELECTRIC MACHINES

Make sure the plug is fitted with the correct fuse, and keep a check on the condition of the power lead and extensions, looking out for cuts and splits, and replacing as necessary. Keep electric machines out of wet conditions. Children and onlookers should be kept well back, out of harm's way.

It is vital to read the instruction manuals that come with these machines before you actually start routing, because not only do they give you good tips on how to use the machine, but they also point out the safety features and safety factors of your particular machine. All routers will vary slightly, either with regard to the plunging mechanisms, or the knobs, locking handles, depth stops, collets, and the numerous other things there are on routers.

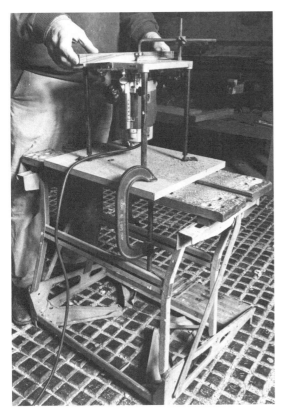

Fig 33 Here the router table is cramped to the WorkMate, allowing work to be carried out at a comfortable height.

Remember to feed cables and dust-extraction hoses out of the back of the table, out of your way, keeping the floor area safe.

Knots

You may not be aware that you are routing through a knot, but if the knot is loose you might end up with a very large chunk of wood flying out, and quite often these will have very sharp edges on them. It is not a nice idea to think of one of these hitting you in the face!

Know where the on/off switch is!

Fig 34 Make sure the router switch faces towards you, not around the back of the table.

THE WORKSHOP SET-UP

The bench height must be right for you! The aim is to be able to work at the bench for long periods without suffering back pain. Unfortunately, this is not always possible, because of the different operations that need to be done on the bench – ideally, we could use a variable-height bench, but in the real world, it will usually have to be a compromise.

The Work-Bench

My own work-bench has a 2in (50mm) thick top, which is 74in (1,880mm) long and 35in (900mm) wide. The legs and frame are made from timber 4in (100mm) by 2in (50mm); the bench needs to be solid and stable. The top overhangs the frame at each end, so that the frame does not interfere with the use of G-cramps. At the right-hand end there is a greater overhang, so that the end vice does not intrude into the frame, weakening it.

When I did my apprenticeship, I used a work-bench for four years with a tool-well in the back of the top. I was not very good at keeping this clean: I would end up with the well filled with tools, wood-dust and shavings. I felt I was spending more time finding my pencil than getting on with the job, so when I made my present bench, I left out the tool-well. I have now been using this bench for about fifteen years; improvements have taken place along the way, some to facilitate certain jobs and some because I felt they would improve the quality of my working life.

As a furniture maker who makes mainly one-off pieces and the odd piece of joinery, I have tried to make my bench handle any situation I might come across. The bench is fitted with two quick-release woodwork vices. One, on the front left, is a Record 52½E, and the other is a tail vice. On the right-hand end is a Record 52D with a metal 'dog', which slides up or down to enable the cramping of work-pieces against a Hex-head bolt which is dropped into holes drilled along the length of the bench top.

Looking at fig 35, you can see that in the left corner of the vice I have drilled a hole, into which I can drop a ¼in (6mm)

Fig 35   Tail vice, showing vice dog and bolts in the bench.

Fig 36   A door held in a side vice and supported on a bolt in the bench leg.

bolt; this has a counterpart along the bench top. These two are for delicate work, which is held near to the front edge of the bench. I use this tail vice and bolt arrangement as much as, or possibly more than, the front vice, certainly for routing, as the tail vice holds carcass sides, book-case sides, shelves, or any flat boards which I am routing, with the router base working off the face side. The vices are set up at these particular ends because I am right-handed; if you are left-handed, you may consider setting them up the other way around. A point I must mention is that I use wood-packers between the bolt heads and the work-piece, to avoid damaging the work in hand, because, by the time it is being worked on the bench, it is already machined to size. I could not then afford to chop off any damaged sections.

By means of a series of holes drilled up the front edge of the right-hand leg, I can put a long bolt in the appropriate hole, which will then support a table top, or, as in fig 36, a full-size door, which is then

clamped firmly in the front vice. This makes it easy to work on the edge of whatever I happen to be working on, as it is at a comfortable height for me. Similarly, the drawers in the bench become supports for smaller items when needed.

The drawers add weight to the bench, making it more stable, as well as keeping the tools in them instantly to hand. To give some idea of the weight of the tools in the drawers, it takes two of us to lift up the drawer unit to carry it out to the van for site work!

Tools

Also hanging above my bench are two quick-release cramps, which are readily to hand when required. All of my hand tools that are likely to be used on a day-to-day basis are within easy reach of my bench. In most cases work-pieces are held in vices or on the bench by quick-release cramps.

Lighting

Lighting is also very important. You must be able to see what you are doing clearly; for the sake of safety and comfort, my bench is well lit by natural light from a window at the back of my bench, backed up by two fluorescent strip lights positioned above the bench, and at 90 degrees to it. I have played around with the lights in different positions to get the best result possible, in an effort to reduce the shadows created when leaning over the bench. As a result, they have ended up

Fig 37 The author's bench and lighting conditions in the workshop.

directly over the two main places on which I work. Having two lights means that one counteracts the shadows created by the other when I am working directly under it.

Power

I have a double 13-amp power point, fixed to a ceiling joist roughly centrally over my bench. To bring the power supply within comfortable range, I have a short extension lead hanging from this socket for plugging in portable hand tools. When this lead is not in use, it is pushed back out of the way into a clip on the end of a tool rack on the wall behind the bench.

4 Materials

You can rout all wood-based materials, plastics and some soft metals. In this book I am staying with wood, since my experience with plastics and metals is extremely limited. I shall only say that special cutters are made for the latter materials.

Solid wood cannot be categorized into simply softwood and hardwood. Each species of timber has its own benefits and disadvantages in being routed; only by being informed by someone who has had experience of routing that particular wood or by having your own hands-on experience of using that timber before (with that particular router cutter, taking into account grain patterns and direction of grain when the timber is being worked), can you have any idea of what to expect.

Remember the exceptions to the rule!
- Not all softwoods are soft, for example yew
- Not all hardwoods are hard, for example balsa

What follows are, I hope, some helpful hints of what can be expected when routing particular woods, drawn from my own experiences.

SOFTWOOD

By definition you might think that being called soft, this wood would pose no problems as regards routing, but it can, albeit not very big ones.

The cutter will work through the wood easily without your having to push too hard, which, in some cases, can give you the false impression that all is going well; when you actually look at the groove however, you may see that its edges are jagged because bits have splintered off, or that the sides are furry. This indicates incorrect feed speed, usually too fast: slow down the rate at which you push the cutter through the wood.

End grain will break out easily when routing across boards, so if necessary,

Fig 38   Breakout at a corner of solid wood board.

Fig 39   Feathering along the top edge of a rebate on end grain. The overshoot batten in the background is to prevent breakout (as in fig 38) occurring.

support the edge of the board with a waste piece of timber to overshoot into. Shear cutters will help reduce both this problem and the feathering on the top edges of grooves.

One sticky problem that builds up is resin on the cutter; softwood has a lot of sap and resin pockets in it. This is exacerbated by the cutter getting hot, so, after a lot of use in softwood, you have to clean off the resin with a solvent. Be very careful about cleaning the bearing on cutters: try to use a minimum amount of solvent so that the grease in the bearing is not dissolved. If you think this *has* happened, I would suggest standing the bearing in machine oil and leaving it for a while, to allow the oil to get into the bearing; remember to wipe off any surplus oil so that it does not get transferred on to the wood when next in use.

All types of cutter (HSS, TC or STC) will work well on softwood provided they are sharp.

HARDWOODS

These can be divided roughly into two groups. Most English and many foreign hardwoods don't cause too much of a problem, apart from being hard and therefore slow-going as regards rate of progress, and maybe suffering a slight burning on end grain. However, some American and African hardwoods, such as teak and iroko, are extremely oily and gritty. This blunts the cutters very quickly, especially HSS (high-speed steel), so you should use tungsten cutters.

The dryness (moisture content) of solid wood is a factor to remember – air-dried timber will be more pleasant to work with, in that you get shavings from the cutter with less dust; kiln-dried timber, if dried to an extremely low moisture content, will produce more dust than shavings.

> Air-dried timber contains about 16–20 per cent moisture. Kiln-dried contains 8–15 per cent.

This is a general overall picture of hardwoods. Each species of wood has its own complex grain structure. Some will rout better along the grain than others and some will, in fact, rout just as well across the grain. Some will also be more suitable for moulding than others.

> Adjusting feed speed (the rate at which you push the cutter through the wood) and motor speed will help to produce a better finish, and to increase the life of the cutter. You can only successfully put this technique to use when you have experience of working with any particular type of wood, and of experimenting with the feed and motor speeds. The optimum speeds will vary with the size of the cutter, because of the outside peripheral speed.

MAN-MADE BOARDS

MDF (Medium-density Fibreboard)

This material really comes into its own for the router enthusiast. It routs easily and cleanly, and gives a good finish on edges, but it does produce a horrible amount of dust, which is harmful to the lungs; so when using MDF it is not just eye protection that is important, but nose and mouth too! Where MDF becomes really useful is in the making of jigs (*see* Chapter 6).

Ply

Ply is easy to rout but it does destroy cutters at a fair rate, even tungsten cutters. If you are cutting to the full depth of your board, and the cutter is set at the same depth for a long period of use, it will wear away the cutter unevenly to the point where you end up with a serrated edge on the cutter. This is because ply is made up of alternate layers of wood, so that you always have end grain and side grain, plus the glue in between the layers. To make the cutter last longer, it is worth altering the depth of the cut every now and then.

Chipboard

Chipboard is easily routed, but it produces dust; also, it is not that uncommon when routing chipboard to see the odd spark coming off the cutter. This is usually because of a piece of metal or stone in the board. In some cases it may take a nick out of your cutter, but despite this, because of the materials that go into the making of chipboard, use only the more expensive tungsten cutters if you want them to last.

The materials mentioned above are by no means all that are available, but are the most common in day-to-day use. If you can successfully handle these, then the others will not give you any problems.

QUALITY OF TIMBER

This section should more accurately be headed, 'the quality of your *machined* timber'. Nearly all work done with the router is on already prepared wood, or man-made boards, so it is important to ascertain how accurately the timber has been machined. This is either down to you, if you do your own machining, or to the timber merchant or yard that supplied the timber prepared, if you buy it pre-machined, as with a lot of softwoods and hardwoods, especially to your order.

In a lot of cases, like cutting joints, it is important to be aware of how accurate the sizing of timber to be jointed is before you start; rather than being able to work off both faces of your wood, you may have to stick to the good old traditional way of working off face sides and edges, which in turn will increase the extent to which you may have to set up the router.

While we are on the subject of solid wood, it is always wise to be aware of what state the timber is in, with regard to dryness (moisture content). This, I know, is a bit of a minefield, for several reasons: you have to take on trust the merchant who sells you the timber, as he, in his turn, is dependent on his suppliers, and so on. Then there is the local saw-mill, which converts whole trees into boards, which will be green and wet, unless the timber has been stacked up to dry for several years, or has been dried in the saw-mill's own kiln.

When you buy timber from a reputable company, they should have a moisture meter that the timber can be tested with to show you how dry the timber is at that point. Then it is up to you to decide what course of action to take, bearing in mind where the timber is going to be once you have made your project. If it is an outside project, then air-dried to about 16–20 per cent moisture will be fine (the timber will only be as low as 16 per cent at the end of a hot, dry summer, and is generally at 18–20 per cent normally). If it is going into a highly centrally-heated home, then to limit the amount of movement that may take place in the timber as it dries out further in this environment, it would be advisable to buy kiln-dried timber with a moisture content in the region of 8–15 per cent, depending on how dry the room is that the piece of furniture (or whatever) is going to be in.

Storing Wood

An important factor, which is quite often overlooked, is the way in which the timber is stored while the project is being made. If it is a big project, or if it is being made in your spare time, you need to keep the timber dry, or at least store it so that it does not cup, twist or bend while the job is in progress. This will depend a lot on conditions in your workshop – whether it is damp, or heated and dry. You can give yourself a lot of problems by not looking after your timber correctly. The most obvious mistake is to stack timber directly on a concrete floor; if the floor has no damp-proof course, the concrete may be very damp. This damp-

Fig 40   Timber being stored in sticks while waiting to be worked on. The photo is deceptive in that the boards are only ½in (12mm) thick and about 16in (400mm) long! They are drawer sides awaiting jointing.

ness will be absorbed by the timber and will make the board 'cup', which is caused by the side on the floor taking in moisture while the other side remains drier.

The best way to store wood safely is off the floor, and with sticks in between the boards to allow air to circulate around all the faces of the wood, thus preventing uneven moisture take-up, or the wood drying out on one side and not the other. If your workshop conditions are good, and your timber is properly dried, then standing the boards on end against a wall, with gaps in between the boards, may well be adequate.

Man-made boards may also take in moisture if they are left standing on edge on a damp floor for a period of time, so a bit of accurate checking of the thickness of the edge that was on the floor, compared with the one that was up in the air, will be worthwhile.

Solid wood will always move to a lesser or greater extent, depending on the moisture content (dryness) of its environment, and how it has been dried. If it was badly kilned there may be pockets of water locked in the wood, which, when opened up by being sawn or deeply grooved or rebated, will release the tension in the wood, so that it could distort. Also, different species of timber react in different ways; some will shrink and expand more in size, and more quickly, than others. In time, and given the right conditions, the wood will stabilize to the environment into which the finished product is to be placed.

5 Using the Router

The processes described in this chapter are some ways of using the router to do common operations; these are not law, but some methods I use myself. Other router users have their own ways and ideas on using a router, and so will you; if not at the moment, then at a later date.

PREPARING THE ROUTER

Fitting a Cutter

Before starting, make sure the router is unplugged. Select a cutter with the appropriate shank size for your machine. If you are using a big router and a small-diameter cutter, then you will also need to use a collet reducer, with which you will have been supplied, or which you may have had to buy as an extra.

Fig 42 A collet being undone with two spanners. The spanner nearest to the motor holds the shaft still, while the other spanner slackens the collet.

Fig 41 Collet reducers with cutters with different sized shanks: ¼in (6mm), ⅜in (8mm), ½in (13mm).

To fit the cutter into the router, you will need either one or two spanners, as supplied with the router. With two spanners, one will be to hold the shaft of the router still, while the other is for tightening, or undoing, the locking nut of the collet. Where there is only one spanner, you will have a built-in spindle-locking device, which you push with your fingers

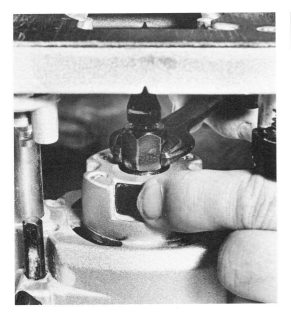

Fig 43 Undoing the collet with only one spanner; the finger is pushing in the spindle-locking device.

Elu routers have a double-locking safety collet, which means that when you loosen the collet nut, it goes slack and then tight again. At this point the cutter is still locked in, so you still have to loosen the nut once more with the spanner before the cutter comes loose.

around, or into, the spindle shaft of the router, to hold the spindle still. The one spanner is then all that is required to move the locking nut of the collet.

Insert your cutter into the collet, almost to the maximum length of the shank available, but not quite – leave two to three millimetres of clear shank visible: at no point should the collet be tightened on to the cutters, or where the cutter has been ground away to form the cutting edges. Tighten the collet-locking nut securely and safely, taking care not to over-tighten it, as this will damage the collet and possibly also the cutter shank.

To release the cutter, simply undo the collet-locking nut until it is slack, and then pull the cutter out with your fingers.

In theory, of course, the cutter never becomes stuck in the collet, nor does the collet get stuck in the spindle, but, I am afraid to say this is the real world and it does sometimes happen, usually on the bigger collet routers. The way I have got over the problem is by undoing the locking nut fully, so that it comes off the spindle, bringing the cutter and, hopefully, the collet with it, then gently tapping the cutter out down through the collet. If this fails, or both are still in the router, then after loosening the locking nut, I resort to putting two large screwdrivers in between the locking nut and the top edges of the cutter, one each side, and gently levering down on them. This may result in the top edges of the cutter being chipped off by the screwdrivers, if it is a solid or a tungsten-tipped cutter, but as yet I have not come across a better way of getting out jammed cutters.

Once you have got the cutter out, try to determine what caused it to stick. Was it you, or someone else, over-tightening the collet, or is there a fault on the cutter shank or in the collet itself? It may just need a good clean, or it may be time for a new collet set.

Read your router manual for instructions on fitting the cutter.

Fig 44 Persuading a jammed cutter to come out of the collet.

Setting the Depth for Straight Cutters

Setting the depth of your cutter is the next job after fitting the cutter into the router. In many cases, you will need a gauge line marked on to a piece of timber, which is held in the vice; then plunge your cutter down until the bottom of the cutter is in line with your gauge mark.

Then lock the router at this position with the locking knobs on the machine. While it is locked in the plunge mode, set the depth-stop device on your machine down to its stop position. Once the stop is set, you may release the router from its plunge mode: the depth is now set.

Depth stops will vary from make to make, but in most cases there is a bar held in position by a thumb screw; when

Fig 45 Setting the cutter depth by lining up the cutter with the gauge line on the timber.

Fig 46   Setting the cutter against the actual object that the cutter depth is being set for.

the thumb screw is released, a bar slides up and down. The bottom of that bar comes to rest on either a turret stop, which is itself adjustable, having two or three stop positions, or the bar on the base of the router itself. The turret-stop device is there so that, if you wish, you may set up two or three different depth settings prior to cutting; either to help you work down to your final depth in equal stages, or for use in cutting recesses that have two levels, such as cabinet locks.

Another way of setting the depth of the cutter is to turn the router upside-down, push the base down with your hand until the cutter projects through the base to line up with what you are setting the depth for (such as a brass hinge), lock at this position, then slide down the

Fig 47   Lining up the cutter flush with the base, ready to set the depth using the depth stop.

Fig 48   The depth can be set with known-size spacers, once the cutter has been set flush with the base.

depth stop to the stop position (*see* fig 46). Another way might be to set the base level with the cutter, lock in this position, and set up the depth stop by means of known-size spacers. Alternatively you can make yourself some sort of setting device with marked increments on it. Even a short, straight piece of wood, with a gauge line marked on it, will be very quick and easy to see, especially if you turn the router upside-down to eye up the cutter against the gauge line.

Setting the Depth for Shaped, or Moulding, Cutters

This can often be done in the same way as setting the depth of straight cutters if the cutter has a point that you can use as a fixed reference point. If not, it is a case of setting the depth by plunging the cutter into a spare piece of wood, and testing to see if you have judged the depth of cut to be what you want.

> The use of a test piece for a sample rout is always worthwhile, before you cut into the real job.

Setting the Router Fence

The fence is used to guide the router parallel to an edge. The distance needs to be set by you, either by measuring from the cutter to the fence with a steel rule, or some other measuring device, or by plunging the cutter to rest just above

Fig 49   Setting the side fence distance from the edge of the cutter with a steel rule.

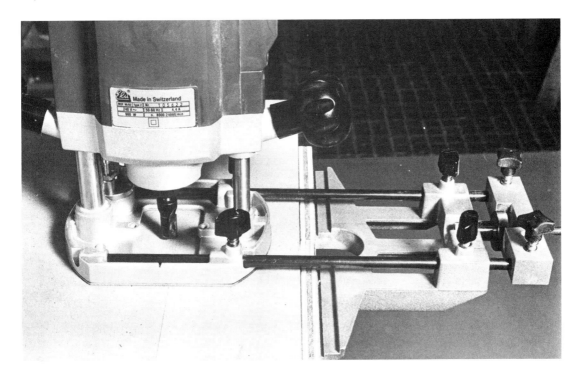

Fig 50   Setting the side fence distance by lining up the edge of the cutter against
the gauge line on the timber.

55

your timber. In this case, you will have to mark a gauge line from the edge to the required distance in from the edge, then rotate the cutter by hand to line up the cutter blade with the line, hold this position and then slide the side fence up to the timber; then lock the fence into position, making sure that you lock all the fence thumbscrews! Do your test run to check. If it is not quite right, then isolate the router and adjust slightly; if the fence has a fine adjuster this will be simple; if not, just a bit more care is needed, that's all.

> Always let the router run to full speed before plunging the cutter into the wood!

CONTROL OF THE ROUTER

It is important that you have firm control over your router, both for your own safety and to enable you to produce good-quality work with the router. Being able to stand up straight, and having your work at a comfortable height to work on helps, as does being able to plunge the router down smoothly and under control. This is important, and means that you need to be able, as far as possible, to put even pressure on both handles.

When I am using the router as a hand-held tool, I rarely lock it into plunge mode. In most situations I am able to plunge down and hold the router down on the stop, which I have already set to the final depth. Unless the depth setting is very shallow, I always cut the groove

Fig 51   Using the router to cut a groove, controlling the depth by using the left hand to hold the side fence as well as the router handle.

(or whatever) with several passes, each pass a few millimetres deeper than the last. This way, I find I can control the plunging quite easily by holding the router in conjunction with the fence.

In fig 51, you can see my left-hand fingers are hooked under the fence, and my thumb and forefinger are holding the side handle of the router. In this way, I can close up my hand, and gauge the amount I plunge the router by. The depth of cut I do in one go is also judged by the amount of noise produced by the router when it is plunged into the wood. If I feel I am taking too much, because of excessive noise or vibration, I can relax my left hand to allow the router to rise up a fraction; conversely, if I feel I could cut more deeply than I am, I close up my left hand, with a bit of help from my right, thereby increasing the depth of the cut. Also, my left hand is gently pushing the fence in against the wood, though in theory this is not necessary: because I am feeding the router by pulling it towards me, the rotation of the cutter is pulling the fence towards the wood in any case.

In the situation in fig 51, if I were to push the router away from me, I would need a lot more pressure to keep the fence against the wood, hence the importance of feed direction. The resulting con-

sequence can be seen in fig 52. The router cutter has drifted off course, out of the groove line, and has pulled itself right out through the side of the piece of wood, making a mess of what should have been a simple operation, running a groove. It is, of course, possible to run a groove in the wrong direction, if you use extreme force in pushing the fence in against the timber and make shallower cuts.

Feed Direction

The general rule is that feed direction should oppose the rotation of the cutter. This is not always possible, and in some

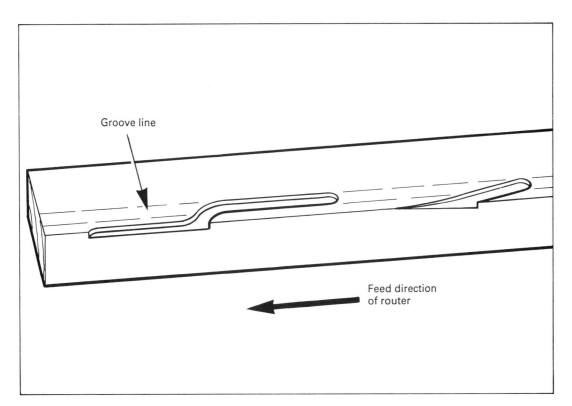

Fig 52　This is what could happen if the router is fed in the wrong direction while cutting a groove near the edge of the timber. The cutter has been forced out of the intended groove line by the rotational forces of the cutter and motor.

situations I can say that to feed the router in the wrong direction can be an advantage. We will deal with this later.

Explaining what happens with regard to feed direction is not easy. Nor is it going to make a lot of sense without you actually using the router and feeling what happens. The rotational force of the motor turning the cutter is one force, and the geometry of how the cutter bites into the timber is another; then there is also the direction in which you are pushing or pulling the router, which is another factor. The router cutter, when in contact with the timber, will want to cut into the wood, and to pull itself along in a certain direction, though not necessarily the direction you want it to go!

These forces are produced by the router, and need to be controlled, or put to good use. If you feed the router in one direction, it will pull at an angle one way, and if you pull or push the router the other way, it will pull in the opposite direction. Or, to put it another way, the forces will pull the fence in against the wood if the feed is correct, or force the fence away from the wood if the feed is from the wrong direction.

The feed direction, for the outside edges of a board, must be anticlockwise (*see* fig 53). For inside cuts, the feed direction must be clockwise (*see* fig 54).

With solid wood, not only do you have to remember feed direction, but also breakout on end grain. This will occur at corners A and B in fig 53, if they are not supported by a batten to overshoot into, as shown in fig 56. If you are routing the outside of a board, this can be overcome by the sequence in which rebates are cut: cut across the end grain first; then, when you cut the side-grain rebates, this will cut away any breakout as long as the

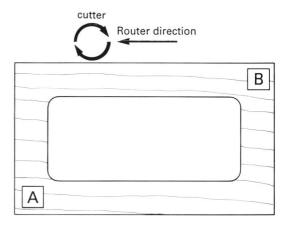

Fig 53 The feed direction of the router for outside edges should be anticlockwise.

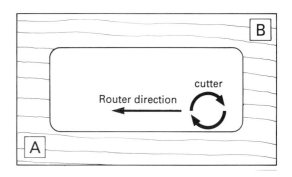

Fig 54 The feed direction of the router for inside edges should be clockwise.

breakout is no bigger than the rebate or moulding that is being cut.

Another method of reducing breakout on end grain is to plunge the cutter to its full depth, with the centre of the cutter in line with the edge of the board, at the corner in which breakout is likely to occur; then run the rebate, or whatever, in the normal way starting, of course, from the other end of your projected run.

When routing the internal edge of solid wood, the problem is not quite the same. If you have rounded inside corners, it is not so much breakout that is the

Fig 55   Breakout on the end grain of a board. Note the slight feathering on the top edge.

Fig 56   There is no breakout on the end corner because of the support batten, and no feathering on the top edge of the board because a Trend sheer-down cutter was used.

Fig 57 Another method of stopping breakout at the end corner of a board is to plunge the cutter centrally in line with the edge of the board before cutting the rebate, then, starting from the end not visible in the picture to cut the rebate.

problem, but the end grain on the rounded corners as at points A and B in fig 54. The fibres could be torn out and left rough, and there is a possibility of burning. You will also notice, when you are feeding the router around at these two points, that there is more resistance to the cutter. If you are cutting a groove across the grain, and only using a straight edge to run the router against, you must again work out in which direction you need to feed the router. In one direction the pull of the cutter will hold the machine against the straight edge; the other way it drifts away from the straight edge (*see* fig 58).

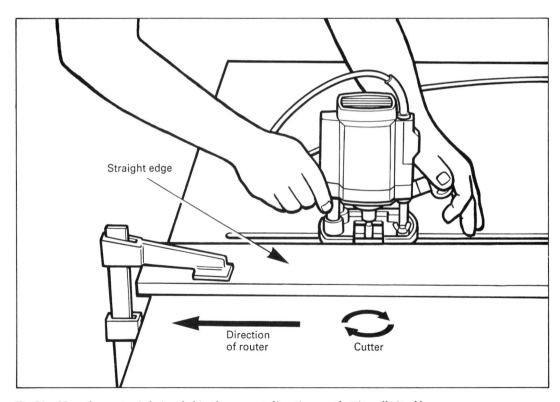

Straight edge

Direction
of router

Cutter

Fig 58 Here the router is being fed in the correct direction, so that it pulls itself against the straight edge; if fed the opposite way, it would want to drift away from the straight edge.

Fig 59   A close-up of breakout on the side grain. This happens with some wild-grained timbers, or when the router operator cuts too much too fast.

Back Cutting (or Running the Router the 'Wrong' Way)

Using this to your advantage can get over the problem of, say, bits of wood splintering off the bottom edge of rebates, as in fig 60. Here, the pencil is pointing to a place where the wood has splintered out. To get over this, you need to set the router up to the full depth of your rebate, but only cut in from the side a very small amount, say ¹⁄₁₆in (1–2mm), as in fig 61. Then you can carry out the remainder of the operation, cutting a groove in the usual way (*see* figs 62 and 63).

Fig 64 shows the three stages involved in cutting a rebate, to overcome the problem of untidiness and jaggedness. This method can be used, if necessary, to cut mouldings.

Fig 60   The pencil is pointing to breakout on the bottom edge of a rebate. This is not desirable, but has happened because of the nature of the grain in the timber.

Fig 61   To avoid side-grain breakout, the first cut is a shallow sideways one done by running the router in the 'wrong' feed direction at the full depth of the rebate (back cutting).

Fig 62   For the second cut, the router is fed in the 'correct' (normal) direction.

Fig 63   For the third cut, the router is again fed in the 'correct' (normal) feed direction.

Fig 64   All three stages of the process of avoiding side-grain breakout shown together.

Fig 65   Two methods of cutting a rebate along the straight edge of a board: one using a side fence and a straight cutter, the other using a rebate cutter with the appropriate-sized bearing fitted to give a correctly sized rebate.

While on the subject of cutting rebates, I would like to mention that simple rebates can be done either with a straight cutter and fence, or a rebate cutter with a bearing fitted, of appropriate size, to produce the correctly sized rebate.

Fences

The use of continuous fences fixed on to the router fence, helps improve the control and ease of use of the router. As in many common operations done with the router, the cut-out in the middle of the fence is not necessary, and, in a lot more cases is actually a nuisance, as can be seen in fig 66. The standard fence is capable of 'falling' around the ends of a board, which will produce a wobbly start, and end too, to the rebate you are cutting. The fence in the background of fig 66 has been set up with a piece of ply to stop what is happening to the fence in the foreground of the picture.

Fig 67 shows a selection of fences that have had plates screwed to them to make using the router easier and safer. With the use of the very long fences in the background, it is possible to run the router past cut-outs in a board without problem. The very back fence in the photo is wide as well as long, which will help keep the router at 90 degrees if the router itself is balancing on a narrow work-piece. As

Fig 66   A standard side fence may fall around the end of a board (foreground);
a side fence fitted with continuous ply facing to close up the centre gap (background), will reduce this problem.

Fig 67   A selection of side fences fitted with wood facing strips to make using
the router easier. The one in the front left is the standard fence unimproved!

these fence plates are either solid wood, ply or MDF it does not matter about cutting into them with the router cutter.

There are some situations where you will have to run the side fence off the opposite edge to the face edge or back edge of the timber to where the router cutter is working, for one reason or another. In most situations I have come across, it is when something has been made, or partly made, and a rebate or moulding has been forgotten before gluing up. This operation is easily done, so long as you remember in which direction to feed the router! It must be fed in the opposite direction to normal use (back cutting). The force of the cutter will pull the fence in against the wood, but be careful when taking big cuts or removing large amounts of timber in one go: the router will want to run away with itself as the cutter eats into the timber.

If you look at fig 69 you will see what happens if you run the router in the so-

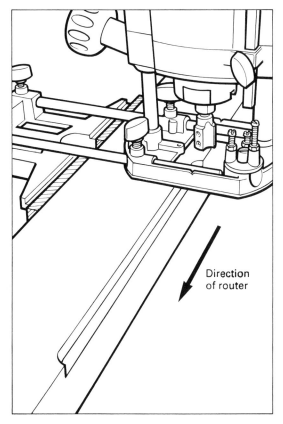

Fig 68　The feed direction of the router when using the side fence off the back edge of the timber. Only small amounts must be cut at a time because the cutter wants to bite into the wood and take itself along.

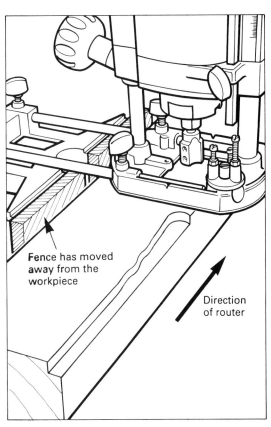

Fence has moved away from the workpiece

Direction of router

Fig 69　The possible result of running the router with the side fence along the back edge of the timber, if you feed the router in the correct feed direction! The cutter will want to force the fence away from the timber, making the rebate wobbly and increasingly wider.

called normal, or correct, feed direction, with the fence set at the back of the timber. You can see the rebate becoming wider as the router progresses along the wood; the fence has been forced away from the timber. If you are strong enough, you can put a lot of pressure on the router to keep the fence against the timber, in order to counteract the forces set up by the cutter. However, I feel that the best thing to do is to make use of these forces to make the job easier for yourself, rather than to fight against them.

HOUSINGS

These are simple and easy to make with a plunging router. All you need is some way of guiding the router, usually across the board width. Shop-bought guide bars are available in different forms, and some router tables can also be set up for this operation. This jig is probably the most used in the workshop on a day-to-day basis.

The form of jig I use for cutting housings consists of two parallel bars, which are held apart at the exact width of the router base by two more bars at each end; these also keep it set at 90 degrees, as in the form of a T-square. The left jig in fig 70 will span 18in (450mm) and has been in use for some fifteen years now, and the other is capable of spanning 36in (900mm). You can also use a similar method of guiding the router, which uses parallel bars set apart the distance of a guide bush; I find this harder to set up because of the lack of visibility, and also because of the difficulty of cramping on to the work-piece. The advantage of running the router between two bars is that

Fig 70   Two parallel guide bars for guiding a router across boards, made from ply.

it is always kept in line; it cannot drift off, as is the case when using a straight edge if you forget about feed direction!

Setting the jig up is simple: you just need to decide which way you want to do this. The use of a marker block is one way. The marker block fits exactly between the bars, with (in the case of my block) a centre line marked, which is used to line up with the centre line of the housing, marked on the work-piece in fig 71; alternatively, lines can be drawn on, set to the distance of your most frequently used cutters; these can be seen on the other side of the marker block in fig 72.

In fig 73, the jig is held in place by two quick-release cramps, which also, when tightened, hold the work-piece down to the bench securely.

Fig 71   Centring parallel guide bars with the centre line of the housing marked
on the board with the centre line of the marker block.

Fig 72   A marker block for guide bars, using a ½in (12mm) housing width, with
½in (12mm) lines centred on the marker block.

Fig 73   Using the router in the parallel guide bars to cut a housing at 90 degrees across a board.

If your housing goes right across the board, then there is no need for stops – it is just a case of starting at one end and working your way through; but in a lot of cases, stopped housings are needed. Stops could be fitted at either end of the housing, or somewhere across the board width. Stops can be set up, if you wish, in a number of ways: for example, battens can be cramped in the right places, or screwed across the bars. In many cases, just lines, marked where you need to stop, will do, as long as you can see them clearly. With the router set in between bars, plunging is a relatively safe operation. The more you use a router, the more accurate you will become with it.

The jig shown in fig 73 can also be used to cut housings that are angled across the board; the main limitation here is the span of the board, but it would not take many minutes to make a set of parallel bars, with the end spacing bars fixed at the required angle for the job. Or, as in fig 74, a bar can be cramped across the parallel bars at the angle required (on left-hand side of photograph). This bar, of course, is then kept against the face edge of the board.

MITRED JOINTS

With the help of the parallel bars, and a

Fig 74   Cutting a housing using the parallel guide bars, but at an angle across the width of the board; the bars are set at the required angle by a batten clamped to them, which then stays set for repeat housings at the same angle.

45-degree chamfer cutter, it is possible to cut perfect mitres on a wide board easily, and with minimal loss of timber. Fig 75 shows the board after being cut across the grain with the cutter, leaving a clean, accurate 45-degree angle, which can then be jointed by means of a spline or loose tongue to make a strong joint.

The groove for the spline can be cut either with a slitter cutter, or a small straight cutter, as in fig 76. Here I have put the two parts to be grooved back to back, to give a right angle, so I can use a fence with the router, to run the groove easily. Also, the router itself has had a piece of perspex fitted in the base opening to reduce the hole size, so that the router will not fall over each end. Fig 77

Fig 75   Using a 45-degree chamfer cutter across the board in parallel guide bars to form a mitred corner joint.

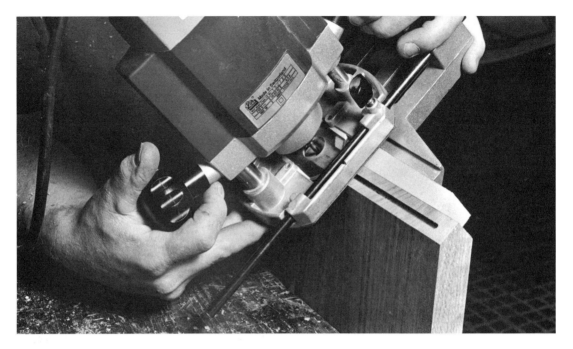

Fig 76   Cutting a narrow groove for the spline to form a joint in the mitre.

Fig 77   The completed mitre with grooves for the spline.

Fig 78   Finished mitre corner. Note the grain following around the corner.

shows the two grooves completed. By turning the router around and working from the other side, I was able to cut both grooves without having to remount the timber in the vice.

MORTISE AND TENONS

The Mortise Hole

The mortise hole is usually made in the narrow face of a piece of timber where a frame, or suchlike, is being constructed. One problem if you are using a router in its portable state, is balancing it on the timber. This can be overcome by the use of two fences set to the thickness of the timber being machined; this also keeps the router cutter in exact line with the mortise hole, and overcomes the direction-of-feed factor.

The point about mortise holes is usually that they need to be deeper than the cutter can go: the average ¼in (6mm) shank router has a cutting depth of about ¾–1¼in (20–30mm), but a number of special cutters with long shanks are available. Also, if you use your router for a lot of mortising, it may be worth getting the special long, spiral mortise cutters that you can buy. Of course, with a ½in (12mm) shank cutter, it is possible to cut a 2½in (60mm) deep mortise hole with a standard straight cutter. It may be possible to work from both sides of your timber if you are making a through mortise hole.

Setting Up

First, select and fit the cutter you wish to use, then set the depth. Set one side fence to give the distance of the mortise hole

from the face side of the timber, and lock, then slide the second fence up to the other side of the timber, and lock. Take care that you don't push the fence into the timber so hard that the router won't slide, or leave it so loose that the router flops about. With the use of two fences set up in this way, you must be sure that your timber is of a consistent thickness; if not, you will have to work with one fence, making sure that you work off the face side each time, and remembering about feed direction.

If you are cutting a mortise hole in the dead centre of your timber, it is worth checking (on a test-piece) to see that it is,

Fig 79   The router ready to begin mortising, using two fences.

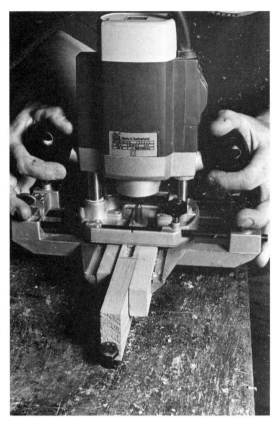

Fig 80   The router cutting a mortise hole.

Fig 81   Two completed routed mortise holes. All that needs to be done now is to square up the ends with a hand chisel.

in fact, the dead centre. Make a small groove with the router and then lift it off, turn it around, and do another groove; the grooves should line up. When you are happy, then you are ready to begin. Once the router is set, all you need to do is mark lines on the timber to show the length of your mortise hole, then just gently switch on the router. Plunge the cutter down just inside one line, work along to the other line, and, stopping just before it, plunge down a few more millimetres, before going back to the other end line again. Continue until the full depth required is reached (if using both fences). If you are using only one fence, once you have completed one length of

the mortise hole, feeding the router in the correct direction, let the router rise up clear and return to the start line to make the next cut. Continue in this way until the full depth is achieved.

Tenons

For the purpose of this exercise, I am working on the principle that we are starting with timber that has been planed all round to produce 2 × ¾in (50 × 18mm) battens, to which we are going to cut a tenon at each end. As the timber came in one long length, we have had to cut it

72

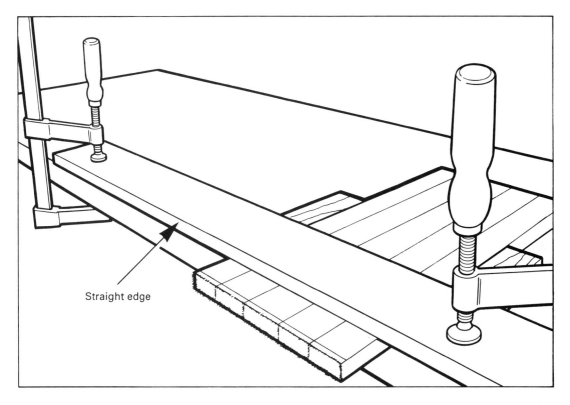

Straight edge

Fig 82   Battens cramped ready with the straight edge set to trim up the ends of the battens.

into short lengths with a hand saw, which is not the most accurate method, but is all that we have, so we will use the router to trim the wood to its final length and make sure it is dead square in both directions. To do this, you need to hold the pieces of wood together side by side, as if you were jointing them together to make one wide board with them, keeping them level with each other.

In fig 82, I have cramped them together, using the tail vice on my bench. It is quite hard to discern, but there are actually five pieces of wood cramped together here (the one nearest to the right-hand bottom corner is, in fact, a waste piece for an over-shoot board, to

prevent breakout). Once cramped together, mark a line across the ends of the pieces of wood at 90 degrees to the edge. This line is for setting up the straight edge to run the side of the router base against. Set the straight edge up parallel with the line to which the router base is going to run, along the straight edge; this line should be the same distance from the edge of the router base as the cutter is. Then set the cutter to cut to just deeper than the thickness of the pieces of wood; now use the router to run along the straight edge, to trim the ends of the pieces of wood. This will give you clean square ends to your battens in both directions.

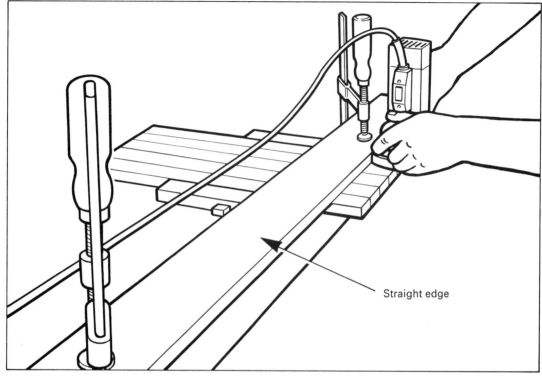

Fig 83 Running the router across the ends to trim up the battens.

At this point, I had better mention that to save setting up and cramping time, it is worth making use of the turret stop on the router: set one depth for trimming the ends, and another to cut the waste material away, to produce the tenons.

The next stage is to remove the straight edge, which was held down by two quick-release cramps, then set the depth of the cutter to take away the waste wood of the tenon. As, in this case, we will be working from both sides of the wood, it is the accuracy of the depth setting that will determine how well our tenon will fit our mortise hole. Set the depth the way you normally would for a rebate, and then on a waste piece of wood, the same thickness as your work-pieces, cut

away across the end free-hand, working on one side, then turning the wood over and cutting away the other side, to test your setting. If you have not set the router up before cramping your work-pieces down, just cramp the test-piece down with a G-cramp at the other end of your bench, to save upsetting the work-pieces already set up. If you are happy with the fit of your tenon in the mortise hole, then fine. If not, then adjust the depth setting – if the tenon is too wide for the mortise hole, then increase the depth of the cutter; or if the tenon is too narrow, reduce the depth of the cut.

Next, set the side fence to the length of the tenon, as we are working back from the ends of the work-pieces to the shoul-

Fig 84   Cutting away the waste to form one side of the tenons.

der line. When this is set, you are ready to cut the waste away, as in fig 84.

Here, I am working from the end free-hand until the last cut, which will be guided by the fence as it runs along the trimmed-up ends, to produce a neat shoulder on the tenon. Once one side has been completed, it is time to uncramp and turn over all the work-pieces: line up the ends and cramp down again. Then cut away the tenon waste on this side. When both sides of one end have been done, you can turn the work-pieces end for end, using the end that has been trimmed and tenoned to line up the work-pieces with, and then begin the process over again, starting with the line and straight edge.

This is just one way of cutting tenons. You may prefer to make a box with a hinged lid, into which your work-pieces slide. This box holds the work-pieces while you run the set-up router across the ends to form the tenons, either with the router in some sort of track, or by means of a guide bush running against the lid of the box, which will produce a straight shoulder line. You may also wish to cut your tenons with the work-piece held vertically, so routing down the end grain, as it were; this can be done holding the router in your hands, as long the router is well supported. However, the length of the tenon is determined by the length of cutter being used, and unless you can back cut at the shoulder line, you could get a lot of breakout at this point. This last method is best suited to a jig such as the WoodRat.

USING THE ROUTER FOR MAKING TRADITIONAL DOVETAILS

Dovetails are used to joint drawer or box sides, for example, or for similar work. These can be hand cut, producing traditional square, sharp dovetails; or machine cut, producing the round inside face of machined dovetails. It will be up to you to decide how much you use your router in the cutting of dovetails: you can use it simply as a fast means of removing waste material, using your hand skills to do the finer part of the job, or use the router to cut them totally, with or without the aid of a jig. Another factor in deciding how much of the job to do with your router will be the number of components you have to make up. The more of the same operation you need to carry out at one router setting, the more efficient will be the overall process.

Using the Router to Remove Waste

To explain what to do, I am going to use the part section of the drawer in fig 85 as

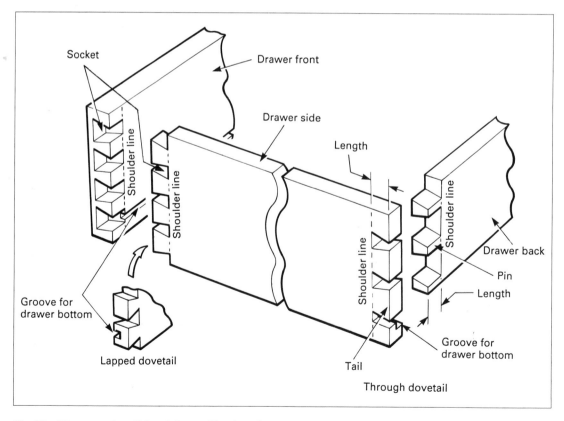

Fig 85   Diagram of traditional dovetailing in a drawer.

an example. First I will try to explain how to cut the dovetails on the drawer side; this side has the part of the dovetail joint cut into it known as the tails, at the front (these are 'lapped' dovetails, and at the other end of the drawer side are 'through' dovetails). One thing I must point out at this stage is the position of the drawer bottom, for if you intend to work to tradition, the bottom groove needs to be located somewhere within the size of the first dovetail. This means that when you make this groove, by whatever means, you will be able to run the cut right through without having to have a stopped groove. Before the days of routers a stopped groove was not an easy thing to do, hence the methods and joints traditionally used in many cases evolved around the tools available to the craftsman at that time.

Back to the dovetails on the front of the drawer *side*: generally speaking, these are quick and easy. To help reduce setting-up time, try to set the spacing of the tails out symmetrically, so that you can work off both edges of the drawer side. One way of cutting out the waste to produce the tails is to mount several drawer sides vertically in a vice, to give you a 'block' of wood, end grain upwards, with all the edges in line. Your drawer sides are now set ready to work on, once the router is set up. Select the dovetail cutter that is appropriate to the size of joint (this is a little restricting, because of the limited range of cutter sizes available – the size of cutter will dictate the sizes of pins), set the depth of the cutter to the distance from the end of the drawer side to the length of the tail (down the length of the grain, to the shoulder line). This depth of cut needs to be locked at this setting, as the last thing you want is for the cutter to

rise up as you are cutting, because of the shape of the dovetail cutter.

Next, set the side fence of the router to your first setting to produce your first cut in the ends of the drawer fronts. When set, you can use the router in the same way you would when taking a rebate, or groove, across a block of wood held in a vice. Of course, you can work with the side fence of the router running off the top and bottom edges of the drawer side, so long as you have set out your tails symmetrically. If not, you will have to work with the side fence running off one edge and will have more fence settings to do. Having finished your cut at that setting, adjust the fence to line the cutter up to the next position. What the cutter is actually doing is taking out the waste wood (socket) in the drawer side, which, in turn, will receive the dovetail pin of the drawer front. For this method you are using the router hand-held.

The sockets for the pins may also be cut by setting a dovetail cutter in a router table, and passing the sides vertically over the table (one by one or several cramped together), using the table fence to set the cutter distance from the edge of the drawer side. One point to note is that as the cutter breaks through the wood, you can get quite a lot of breakout, so a spare side, or packer, to use behind the side is needed so that the breakout does not occur on your actual work-piece.

On the side of the drawer, on the back, there is, as you can see in fig 85, a slightly different arrangement – a 'through' dovetail. Basically, the method of cutting the tails for the back is the same as for the front end of the drawer side, except that a different fence setting is necessary, and possibly also the height of the cutter will have to be changed to allow for the thickness of the back of the drawer, which is possibly different to the setting you had at the front end. Take note of the half pin at the bottom of the back of the drawer side. In most cases you would have to cut this socket by hand, as the bottom-most edge of the socket is parallel to the bottom edge of the drawer side, instead of at an angle. This is because this half pin runs in line with the drawer bottom, as seen in fig 85. If you wish to avoid this problem, then raise up the position of the socket for this pin and make it into a full pin, as for the rest of the joint. This will mean that you will have a shoulder at the bottom of the drawer back (the same as the top edge of the drawer back). You can use this to your advantage by setting out the pins equi-distantly from the top and bottom edges of the drawer side. This will reduce the number of settings needed for the router fence, because it will enable you to run the fence off both edges of the drawer side and also, later, of the drawer back.

Next, we go on to the drawer back. You are now going to cut away the waste to produce the pins that will fit snugly into the tails on the drawer side. For this you will need a straight cutter fitted into your router. The safest way of cutting the pins on the drawer back is by having the cutter projecting vertically up through the router table. The cutter needs to project up from the table to the same distance as the length of the pins to be cut (from the end of the wood to the 'shoulder' line). Also, you will need a block of wood to use to guide the drawer back through the cutter, at the same angle as the dovetail cutter used to cut the dovetails on the drawer side. This means your drawer back is being pushed vertically through the cutter, but at an angle to the

table fence that gives you the distance setting of the pins from the top or bottom edge of the drawer back. This block needs to be big enough, or, rather, have enough contact area with the table and fence, for you to keep the drawer back vertical with the cutter and at the correct angle to the fence when being pushed through the cutter.

This will give you one side of your pin at the correct angle: you need to then turn your guide block end for end to give you the angle for the other side of the pin. As you can imagine, this involves quite a lot of setting of the fence, so you need to assess whether you have enough components to make it worthwhile, to save time, and whether your ability at adjusting the router is better than your hand skills. How accurately you adjust the fence will determine how well your dovetails fit.

Cutting the pin of a lapped dovetail on a drawer front cannot be done totally with the router; some amount of hand work with a chisel is required. It can be made to look like a traditional lapped dovetail from the outside when it is put together, but when taken apart it is soon obvious that it was done by machine, because the inside bottom edge of the sockets will have the same round shape as the dovetail cutter. The best you can hope for is that the router assists you by speeding up the process of waste removal and by giving neat shoulder lines to your dovetails.

You can use the same method to cut out the pins in the laps as you did on the back of the drawer, but you must have a stop set on the table to give the required distance up to the lap. What you will end up with is rounded corners in the tail sockets, which will have to be chiselled

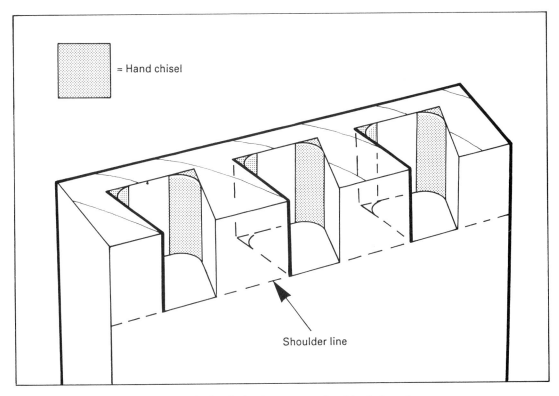

= Hand chisel

Shoulder line

Fig 86   Routed out lap sockets ready for the back corners to be chiselled out by hand. To do this, the router was fixed into a table.

out by hand, as in fig 86. How much you have to chisel out will depend on the diameter of the cutter. This will have to be a compromise: the smaller the diameter of the cutter, the less waste there is to chisel out in the corners, but with a small diameter cutter, you need to make more passes in order to remove the waste in the first place. These methods will produce good tidy dovetails, as long as you take the time to set up the cutters and fences accurately, if you don't have specific dovetail jigs.

Using the Router for fast waste removal

I feel, personally, that by far the best use of the router in traditional dovetailing is merely to serve the craftsman's hand skills by allowing the fast removal of waste and creating neat shoulder lines. By marking and cutting down the grain, by hand, with a knife and dovetail saw, both tails and pins to the shoulder line, I feel that I am keeping up my own hand skills; and also, I have no restrictions on size or spacing of the dovetails, so am able to fulfil my own pleasure at cutting dovetails by hand without external constraints.

Then, using a 2mm straight cutter, set at a depth of just over half the thickness of the drawer sides and backs, and set the router fence at the required distance from the end of the drawer side to the shoulder line of the dovetails. Then cramp the drawer components with the tail vice on the bench, and proceed to use the router to cut out the waste pieces with the fence running off the end of the side, using the saw lines as the start and stopping marks for routing. When doing this, you are in fact using the router in place of the coping saw to cut along at the shoulder lines, as the router cuts and trims in one go. I must point out that with narrow drawers there isn't much to run the fence against,

and that it is worth reducing the opening in the router base with perspex in this case, to give greater support to the router. With practice, the speed and accuracy with which you plunge in and out of the dovetails will improve. The reason for only cutting just over half-way through is that you can then turn the work-piece over, to avoid breakout and to reduce the stress on the 2mm cutter; for example in the case of drawer sides 13mm thick you need to cut to a depth of 6.5mm.

Once you have done the routing, all that remains is to tidy up the bottom corners with a sharp chisel where saw and router have not quite met. When you have cut down the pins of the lap dove-

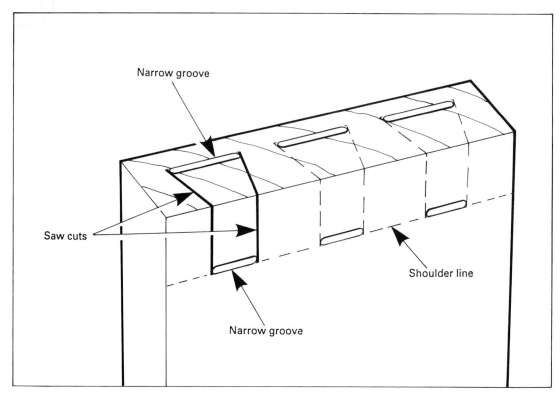

Fig 87 Narrow grooves routed at the shoulder lines to make removal of waste quick and easy with a hand chisel.

tails on the drawer front with your hand-saw, they will be ready for the router. This time you need to set the router up as if you intended to cut a narrow groove with a 2mm straight cutter, set with the side fence running off the end of the drawer front to the shoulder line of the pins, with the cutter set to the depth of your sockets to receive the tails. This will be quite a lot to expect of a small diameter cutter, so you will need to work down to full depth gently, being careful not to break the cutter. Then reset the fence to the distance from the inside face of the drawer front to the shoulder line marked on the end grain (this is the length of the tails). Once set, proceed as before, plunging in and out of the pins: your two narrow grooves should meet at the bottom back corner of the sockets, as in fig 87. The waste will remain in place because you cannot saw right into the bottom corners of the sockets: to finish off, it is just a case of chiselling out the waste as if doing it all by hand. Once you start breaking up the waste in the laps, it soon falls out in chunks, as the back and bottom have already been cut by the router. This will give clean, accurate shoulder lines that should not need to be touched with a chisel.

This method proves that tradition and modern technology *can* work together!

INLAY

Running small grooves for inlaying is a nice, delicate job for the router and a suitable cutter. The inlay in fig 88 is $\frac{1}{16}$in $\times$ $\frac{1}{16}$in (1.5 $\times$ 1.5mm) rosewood. As grooves for inlays are usually shallow, a very short cutter only is needed; this reduces the chance of the cutter breaking. With

Fig 88 Fitting an inlay into a groove. Note the small cutter used to make the groove.

very small diameter cutters, the waste will not clear very efficiently because of the size and chip clearance available to them, so it is often necessary to run the router along the groove a second time to clean out the waste. Care must be taken to gauge the correct feed speed when running the cutter across the grain, because it is easy to get breakout or feathering of the grain on the top surface; this may not seem very drastic, but remember you are working to a very small sized groove.

Inlay in Curved Work

Fig 89 shows part of a groove being routed around a curve. The router is

Fig 89   Routing an inlay line following the curve, using a shaped block by means of a fence.

Fig 90   Putting on the fence block with double-sided tape.

being guided with the use of a waste block, which has a curve cut on one edge to match the curve on the work-piece (the same applies to convex as concave curves). As a very small cutter is used, the force on the fence is minimal, and the guide block is held on to the base of the router with double-sided sticky tape. Alternatively, the block can be screwed to the side fence, which makes it easier to set up the distance of the inlay line.

ROUTING WITH TRAMMEL BARS

Circles and large radii can be cut with the

Fig 91   Here you can see the matching curve of the guide block, with the router held upside-down to demonstrate. Rosewood inlay has been put into the groove to make it stand out.

router easily and accurately using trammel bars. These can also be used to make up complicated patterns, cut into the surface or pierced through the wood to form panels or screens.

We will start with the small trammel bar, which is bought as an extra to your router. This bar locks in the fence rod position on the base of the router. The other end has a pin on the underside, and a hand knob on the top. You set the radius distance from the pin to either the near side of the cutter, for outside radii, or to the far side of the cutter from the pin, for inside radii.

The next step is to provide the centre mark for the router to rotate around. If

Fig 92   Using the router with a trammel bar, one hand holding down the pivot point, the other holding the router.

you can work from the underside, so that you don't have a small pin-hole in the face side of your work-piece, then all well and good; however, in many cases you will need to work from the face surface, so the use of a piece of ⅛in (2–3mm) clear perspex is required, to locate the trammel pin in. The use of double-sided tape is an easy way of fixing down the perspex to the work-piece. The pin in the trammel bar is sufficiently adjustable to take up the thickness of the perspex, in order to keep the router base flat on the work-piece. (A thin piece of board material may be used instead of perspex, if the centre lines are lengthened and lined up with the centre lines on the board.) If you look at fig 92, you can see the perspex, and just make out the double-sided tape underneath it.

Take note that you will need one hand on the trammel-bar end to keep the pin located in its centre mark, and the other hand to operate the router: this is one occasion when the router cannot be held with both hands, unless you are lucky enough to have three hands! As you can see, in fig 92 I have not! I am holding the router at the top of the machine, so that I am able to plunge it down effectively; putting downward pressure on one handle alone is not always an effective method of plunging. When holding the router by the top of the motor, you must hold it in such a way that you do not obstruct air from getting into the motor through the vents; otherwise there is a risk of over-heating.

When cutting full circles, you need to be aware of the power cable, so that it does not get caught up with the router or the trammel bar. (Looking back at fig 92, now, I should have had the power cable coming down from over my shoulder.)

Also, if cutting large radii make sure that both the work-piece and the piece that is coming off are well supported.

Remember the correct feed direction for outside and inside cutting. This may not seem so important when cutting a circle from a board, but it will possibly improve the quality of the edge of the work-piece. Pulling the router in the correct direction will make work easier and the router more controllable. Anticlockwise is the best direction for the outside edge of a circle; for the inside edge of a ring clockwise is best. When trimming a circle that has already been bandsawn out, or when putting a moulding on a circle, you must remember to feed in an anticlockwise direction when using a trammel bar.

There are, of course, other manufacturers' bars available, as described in Chapter 2, though a trammel bar is one of the most easy attachments to make yourself. Any length of board material will do, with a hole cut in one end to receive a guide bush, and a small nail or pin to be used as the pivot point along the board, at your required distance, as in fig 93.

Fig 94 shows a trammel base. This is a false base for cutting circles within the size of the router-base area. The base is made out of a piece of MDF, which has a panel pin protruding through the MDF for the pivot point. The panel pin is set at the required distance from the edge of the router cutter, and this base is held on to the router by two screws. To make the setting-up of the pivot point easy, you can see I have marked lines at the correct distance from the cutter, then drilled a

Fig 93   Home-made plywood trammel bars and a router fitted with a guide bush.

Fig 94   Detail of the trammel base, showing the cutter and pin (pivot point).

fine hole through the MDF with a ¹⁄₁₆in (1.5mm) drill; the panel pin is then pushed through from the top side of the base. Once this base is screwed on to the router base, the pin is held in position by the base of the router. The MDF base is ½in (12mm) thick and a ⅝in (15mm) panel pin is used as a pivot, giving a ⅛in (3mm) projecting pin – cheap and simple.

DRILLING WITH THE ROUTER

The router used as a hand drill has one big advantage over an ordinary electric hand drill, in that the hole will always be drilled at 90 degrees to the surface, in all directions, and will be very clean. The big disadvantages are the lack of visibility in sighting up the cutter with the centre of the hole to be drilled, and the router sliding about, if used free-hand. To help stop the router from sliding about, temporarily fix some abrasive paper (sandpaper) on to the base of the router with double-sided tape; use a medium-grit paper for best results. In many cases, you will be able to use the fence to give your setting for the drill hole in one direction.

If you look at fig 95, you will see the router being used to drill holes for adjustable shelf pegs on a book-case carcass side. The fence is keeping the distance set from the edge of the board, and the drill bit in front of the router is being used as a stop against the router base to set the distance for the next hole.

You can, of course, make your own stops to work from, once your first hole is drilled; for example, you can use a block of wood with a dowel fixed into it, which fits into the previous hole – or the next hole back if holes are close together – at the appropriate distance from the end of the block (*see* fig 96).

Fig 95 Using the router to drill holes for adjustable shelf pegs, using a drill bit to set the spacing of the holes from the edge of the router base.

Fig 96 Block of wood with a dowel for a space block, used for spacing shelf peg holes.

This whole system relies on the first hole being drilled in the correct place, and on your being able to get the first hole of the opposite side of the board in line, so a bit of care is needed on the first hole of each run. Once this is done, drilling the holes up the length of the wood with a router is as quick as using a pillar drill stand, even more so if the piece of wood you are drilling is very big or long: with regard to handling, you must consider whether it is easier to take the wood to the machine, or the machine to the wood.

Cutters for Drilling

Most standard, straight router cutters are capable of drilling holes, as long as they have what is known as 'bottom-cut' design. This means that the cutter has to be made so that it can be plunged down into the wood. These cutters are usually the ones that you are able to buy at your local tool shop, because of the fact that nearly all routers sold are the plunging type. The cutter manufacturers do, of course, make cutters specifically for drilling – refer to your cutter catalogue.

Hinge Hole Recess

By this, I mean the type you see on kitchen cupboard doors, which, in most cases, need a 35mm diameter hole for the hinge body to sit in. Because of the size of the cutter required, a reasonably powerful router is usually needed. Careful setting-up is necessary to cut these holes (*see* fig 97).

To make lining up easy and accurate, use a perspex sub-base fitted to the router. This should have centre lines at 90 degrees to each other, centred on the cut-

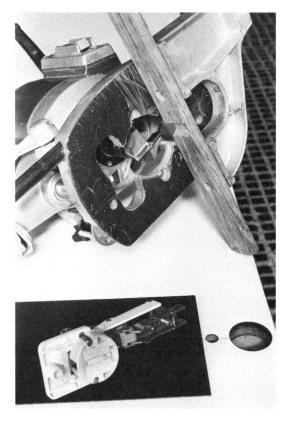

Fig 97   Hinge hole recess and hinge.

ter and scored into the perspex, to use to line up with the centre lines marked out for the position of the hole to be drilled. The side fence can be used to set one distance of the hole from the edge of the door. The other distance will have to be set by lining up the cutter with a centre line where the hole is to be drilled. Once the router is positioned to plunge, G-cramp the router base to the door before starting the router, so that as the cutter makes contact with the surface it is not pulled sideways by the force of the router being started. This way, you will get a clean and accurately placed hole.

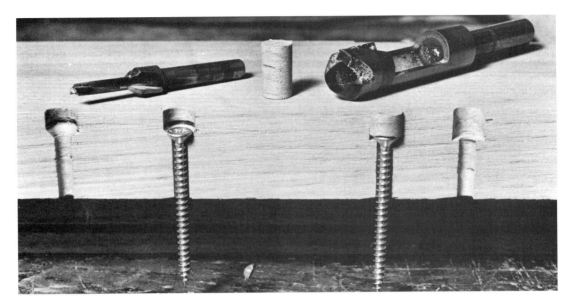

Fig 98   Cross-section showing the use of a combination cutter and a plug cutter. The right-hand screw has a plug fitted (spot the hole on the surface). If the grain on the plug matches well, it can be quite difficult to see.

Drill Combination Cutters

These are cutters that are designed to drill clearance holes; counter-sink and then counter-bore for plug. Fig 98 shows a cross-section of the holes produced by this type of cutter.

SLOTTING AND GROOVING

When using a slotting or grooving cutter on an arbor, you must remember that you cannot plunge the router. The cutter has to be fed in from the end of the wood, or into the wood from the side in the case of stopped grooves. The distance of the groove from the face edge of the wood is set by the router depth stop, and this depth setting needs to be maintained during cutting, so you will need to lock the router into plunge mode. Once the cut is completed and the cutter is out of the timber, you can, of course, release the plunge lock. The depth of the groove itself is set by the relationship of cutter diameter to bearing diameter, so a selection of bearings is required if you make slots at different depths. If you do not have the right bearing for the depth you require, you can increase the size of the bearing by wrapping some layers of masking tape around it, thereby increasing its overall diameter. However, the bearing must be running smoothly, or the masking tape will just become chewed up.

You may find you have to use the router on its side, horizontally; in this case, you have to make sure that the base is in contact with the wood all the time, because if it is not, a wobble could appear in the groove, as in fig 99.

Figs 100 and 101 show the cutting of a

Fig 99   A close-up of a slot that has got a wobble in it.

Fig 100   Running a slot for a weather strip in a door stile section using a slotter.
This is being done on the bench with the router vertical.

Fig 101 Door stile with a weather seal
fitted into the slot.

OVERHEAD ROUTING

This is where the router is fixed in its upright position, suspended over a table on which the work is placed. By means of a hand lever or foot pedal, the router is then lowered on to the work. Advantages are that it holds the router extremely rigid, reducing the amount of vibration, and thus producing a better finish; and because of the visibility of the cutter, making repetitive copying easier and safer. In the centre of the table there is usually a pin, which is directly in line with the centre of the router; this is used for guiding jigs on their correct path, so with overhead routing, the jig or template is mostly under the object to be routed.

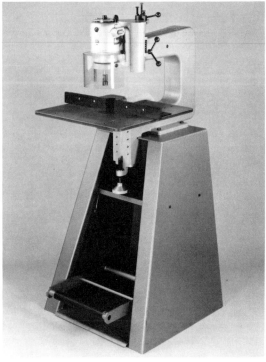

Fig 102 The Trend foot-operated stand
fitted with Elu MOF112 motor.

slot for a weather strip. This is only one use of a slotter. Another use that comes readily to mind is putting grooves in the edges of boards to be butt-jointed up to make a wider board for loose tongues, which can be cut from ply, for example. The slotter cuts through the wood easily and at a faster feed rate than a standard straight cutter, so that in a lot of cases it can be used instead of a standard cutter to produce narrow grooves up to ½in (12mm) wide with a single pass of the router.

90

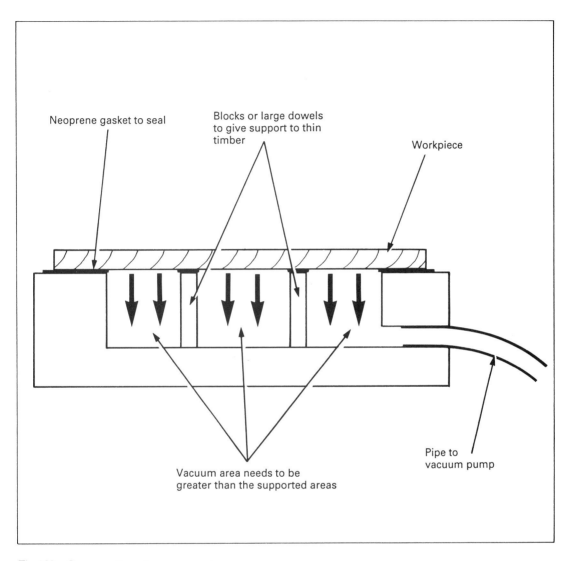

Neoprene gasket to seal

Blocks or large dowels
to give support to thin
timber

Workpiece

Pipe to
vacuum pump

Vacuum area needs to be
greater than the supported areas

Fig 103   Cross-section of a vacuum clamp.

Overhead routing is extremely well suited to the mass production of small irregular shapes. These shapes are either held in shaped jigs, which hold the work tightly, or are held by vacuum clamping. A vacuum clamp is a hollow, flat box, with enough suction to pull the work-piece down on to the box (*see* fig 103). I would not recommend the use of a domestic vacuum cleaner for long periods: you will need to buy a commer-cial vacuum pump.

TABLE ROUTING

At what point you decide to use a router table will be up to you, or will perhaps depend on the type of work you want to do. Many of the operations that can be done with the hand-held router may be carried out with the router table. A conscious decision must be made as to which method you wish to use, taking into consideration safety, ease of working, setting-up time, cutters and accessories available to you, and any other factors that may be relevant.

Using the Router in a Table

By inverting the router and mounting it in a table of one type or another, you greatly increase the number of uses to which a router can be put. As previously mentioned, the type and make of table you use, will be a matter of personal preference. The table I usually use with a router is the Elu E40900 Moulding Kit. This table is relatively small in size, but very adaptable; it comes into its own when the timber to be routed is too small or too awkward to cramp into the vices or on to my bench. The table is used either cramped on to my bench or on to a WorkMate, depending on what type of work is to be carried out.

Fig 104 shows the router and table being used in one of its most simple modes. Putting a chamfer on the corners of a cube of wood, the wood is being passed by the cutter using the bearing as the means of fence or guide: the amount of cut set depends on how much of the cutter is protruding through the table. The projection of the cutter can be set with the router's fine height adjuster; this adjuster does make cutter adjustments easier and more accurate. The plunge-locking device of the router locks the router in its final setting.

Fig 105 shows the router table being

Fig 104   Using a router table to put a chamfer on a small block of wood.

used to trim a small curved rail to its finished size and shape. Notice the use of a bearing-guided trimming cutter. The rail is band-sawn out over-size, to allow for trimming: the outside curve has already been trimmed using the same method, as shown. As you can see, the jig holding the rail is very simple: only two toggle cramps are needed. Not only do these hold the rail firmly in position, but they also provide good handholds on the jig for you to hold the jig with, while keeping the hands safely out of the way of the cutter.

Using the table to mould or rebate and groove straight timber is straightforward.

Fig 105   Trimming a curved rail in a jig on a table using a template profile cutter.

First set your cutter to the required set-ting. When using the table for straight timber, you will in most cases be using the straight fence, which is mounted on the table to run your timber against. On the Elu E40900 kit, a fine sideways adjuster is supplied, so that, along with the fine height adjuster fitted to the router, both adjustments for depth and height of cut are easy to carry out.

Guiding the Wood past the Cutter

The method used for guiding the wood for table routing on such a table will depend on the job in hand and the type of cutter you can use to do the job. Apart from small work done on the table, it is most suited to the shaping or moulding of curved or shaped work. An alternative to using a cutter with a bearing for guid-ing, is to use an independent bearing, fixed to an arm, which can be positioned over the cutter to run directly on the work-piece or against a jig, as in fig 106. This bearing can be positioned in any place over the cutter to set the amount of sideways cut required.

If it is at all possible, the use of pres-sure pads is recommended (*see* fig 107). If both pads are used, then the timber is kept against the table and fence without a problem; but if only one pad is used, because of the size of the timber or, say, an already shaped edge, then more care

Fig 106   The set-up for using a bearing over the cutter, running directly on the work-piece.

Fig 107   Using the pressure pads to keep the work-piece held against the bed and fence of the router table.

Fig 108   A home-made pressure bar, for small sections of timber.

Fig 109   Feeding small sections by hand.

is needed. The thing to get right with the pressure pads is the amount of pressure you put on the work-piece itself: you need enough pressure to hold the work against the table and fence, but not so much that it becomes hard work to feed the work-pieces under the pads (it does help the work-piece to run through smoothly if the pads are kept well waxed up). When the pressure pads are in position, they also act as guards, preventing your fingers from getting too close to the cutter.

If the work-pieces that you are routing are very small, you may need to make your own pressure pad, as in fig 108. This can be a piece of ply or MDF with saw

slits cut into the board. The edge that runs against the work-piece is slightly curved: this makes it possible to get pressure in the right place, and makes it easier to feed the work-piece along, since it guides the work into the fence. As can be seen in the photograph, there is a whole series of saw cuts; these are, in fact, at a slight angle, angled in the direction of feed. They make the board springy and become anti-kickback fingers, because of the way they are angled: when pushed in the wrong direction they will grip the work-piece, preventing it from flying out, if for some reason you lose your grip on the work-piece while moving your hands to a new position.

In fig 109 you can see a small-sectioned piece of timber being moulded. I have to say that this method is not the best way of doing this, but sometimes there is no

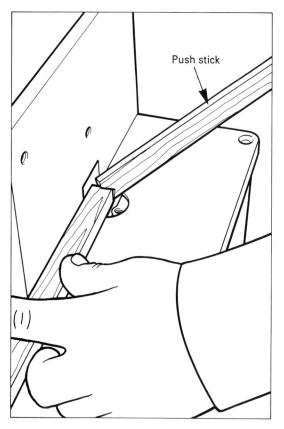

Fig 110   Using a push stick to feed the timber past the cutter safely.

stick end may be chewed up by the cutter – and the push stick can be replaced much more easily than your fingers!

FREE-HAND ROUTING

The use of the router totally free-hand takes confidence and experience, along with a fair amount of strength when cutting away large amounts with big cutters. The use of routers for carving signs, and for putting pictures into coffee tables, and so on, is common place. How much control you have over the router will depend on several things: your skill, your own strength, the power of the router itself, the type and size of cutter, the depth of the cut you are taking at one time, and the grain and the density of the material

alternative. The danger arises when you have to transfer your 'front' hand from the in-feed side of the cutter to the out-feed side, because you will need to move your hand off the work-piece, out around the cutter position and back on to the work-piece to achieve this. This is the point at which most problems occur: if you are not careful, the wood can chatter, or a burn mark may appear where you have stopped to move your hand. To push the end of the work-piece safely past the cutter, the use of a push stick as in fig 110 is *strongly* recommended. The worst that can happen is that the push

Fig 111   Using the router free-hand.

you are routing. The main problem with using the router is stopping it cutting into somewhere you did not intend it to go, hence all the jigs and guides that have been developed and made for the router.

Using a router free-hand is quick and effective for, say, something like a house sign. The smaller the router and cutter, the more control you will have over it. When free-hand routing on solid wood, a lot of concentration is required on the cutter, and you need to beware of the pull of the router when changing the direction of cut. When using the router free-hand to remove the background for carvings, for example, it is best to work from the middle of the waste outwards, taking small amounts at a time and working carefully up to your lines. When you have had a bit of practice, you will be quite surprised at how accurately you can work to the lines. Be patient!

ROUTING PROBLEMS

Fig 112 shows a basic groove in a piece of wood; if you look at it carefully, you will see that the side part looks serrated. This could be for any one of several reasons:

1 The router feed speed is too fast.
2 The cutter is blunt.
3 The cuts taken in one go are too deep.
4 The wood is not cramped firmly enough.
5 The cutter is loose in the collet.
6 The lower shaft bearing on the router is worn out.

In each case, the remedy is obvious.

Fig 112   A badly cut groove. Note the rippled side of the groove and the burn marks.

Altering Router Speed

This will affect the quality of finish the cutter will produce. Fig 113 shows the end grain of a piece of ash wood, which has had an oval cutter run along the end at different speeds, as set on an Elu router. Starting at the left end, the section up to the first arrow was cut with the router speed dial set at 1; then the dial was set at 3, up to the second arrow; next, for the last section, it was set at 5. As you can see, there are no burn marks until the fastest speed was used.

You can obviously only take advantage of altering the speed if your router has variable speed control; otherwise it is up to you to do the best you can by altering the speed at which you, yourself, are feeding the router along the wood.

In fig 114, you can see on the right-hand side on the side grain a big burn mark at the beginning. This was caused by me not concentrating on the router at the time, but talking to the photographer!

Fig 113   Showing the use of different motor speeds to avoid burning on end grain.

Fig 114   A burn mark is visible in the front right corner, indicating too slow a feed speed.

Fig 115   The difference between using a pin-guided cutter and a bearing-guided one.

In this case, the feed speed had been too *slow*.

Burn marks can also be caused by pin cutters, as seen in fig 115. Both cutters are rounding-over cutters; the one in the foreground has a fixed pin to guide the cutter. As you can see, it has left quite a bad burn along the wood, whereas the cutter in the background has left the wood unmarked. Remember that if you are just running a pin cutter along a straight piece of wood, you could always set the cutter up in conjunction with the router side fence; if you line the fence up with the pin of the cutter very fractionally back inside the line of the fence, the fence will run against the wood and not the pin of the cutter.

IMPROVEMENTS TO THE ROUTER

Any small alteration or improvement that you can make to your fence or router base may well be worth the time and effort, if it makes the router work more efficiently and consequently makes life easier for you. In fig 116, the two routers centre and right have had perspex addi-

Fig 116   Three router bases: the one on the left is the standard base, the centre one has had a small perspex piece put on the base to reduce the opening aperture, and the one on the right has had a piece of perspex fitted to the entire base, to make using the router easy. These are temporary improvements.

99

tions fixed to the bases to reduce the cutter opening, which makes using the router easier and safer.

If you look closely at the base of the router on the right, you can see that this has had six small holes drilled through the base, so that other blocks of wood can be fixed on to the base to do specific jobs when necessary. The router is capable of doing many jobs, and can be altered to do even more with a little bit of imagination!

ROUTER MAINTENANCE

The router itself needs very little maintenance; what does need doing is on-going maintenance, in order to keep the router working at its best, and to give you a better time when setting the router up and using it. The plunging rods and fence rods need a small amount of lubricant to keep them sliding smoothly; if you can use a dry lubricant, like PTFE or silicon, you will find this better because dust and shavings don't stick to it.

The router base needs to be kept clean and benefits from some wax polish, as does the fence plate. Blow dust away from the motor air vents and check the vents for shavings, as air has to pass freely through the motor to prevent overheating. Check the state of the power lead and plug at regular intervals; if these get damaged replace them, don't patch!

If sparks are coming from the top of the router, this may mean that the commutator brushes need renewing; this seems to be a rare event, however, on modern routers. The part that most often gives up on a heavily used router is the lower shaft bearing; the bottom part of the router becoming extremely hot, unusual vibration, a higher noise level and slower speed, and the router coming to a stop very quickly and harshly when switched off are all signs of this happening. It is best to get the bearing changed by your local router agent before more serious damage is caused to the router.

The most important check of all, is on the condition of the lock nut and collet. What you are looking for are signs of rounding-over at the collet opening, and pits and score marks on the meeting surfaces of the nut and collet. If there is damage, replace them with a new set. If you look after your router it will be more pleasant to use and will perform what you ask of it more reliably.

6 Jigs and Templates

If you look around in any workshop, you will see funny-looking pieces of wood, or boards with bits fixed on in an odd place, or with holes in them, hung on the walls or stacked up in corners of the workshop. To you they may just look like strange objects and you cannot work out what they are for; but to the person who made and used them, they are extremely important. In fig 117, you can see a selection of jigs, and these are just the ones that I could put my hands on quickly to produce this picture. All of them have at some time fulfilled a useful purpose. Some will be used time after time and some will never be used again, but will languish somewhere until at a much later date someone will make the brave decision to throw them on the fire.

HOME-MADE JIGS

Only you as an individual will be able to

Fig 117 A selection of jigs.

decide whether to buy a commercially made jig, or to spend the time making the jig yourself. In some cases, making the jig becomes part of the challenge of the overall job, and a good learning experience as to how the router works and what is involved in making a good jig. Also, you may need such an individual jig, special to your own particular needs, that the big boys have not yet developed one like it.

In a lot of cases, jigs can be made with no hand-tool skills at all, for if you are keen on machines you can usually invent some way of getting the machine to cut or shape the template for you. Having no hand-tool skills would, however, restrict your jigs to straight edges, circles and radii, parts of an ellipse, or some object that is lying around that you can use as your template. But, with even basic hand-tool skills, you can make whatever shape template you can dream up, with the help of spoke shaves, rasp files, sandpaper and whatever else you can get your hand on to the job. No need to say it, but if you are a skilled craftsman, then the world is your oyster!

Jigs and templates can be in many forms, from a simple straight edge with blocks fixed on for stops, to complicated curved shapes. They all help you to do a better job and make the router more versatile. The most important specification for a jig is that it is absolutely accurate. How you get it to this state will depend on your skill or ingenuity, but the finished jig does need to be accurate because any discrepancies will be copied by the router. In a lot of cases, the making of the jig is more time-consuming than doing the job you have made it for; however, it has made the task in hand possibly safer, certainly easier, quicker, repeatable and idiot-proof.

In most cases, jigs can be made out of odds and ends. Some materials are better than others, though, especially man-made boards, like ply and MDF. Because they remain stable and flat, they can be worked easily. As well as the board, you will need equipment such as screws, nails and glue for fixing; it is also worth remembering things like double-sided tape for temporary fixings – for example, attaching a block on to the base of the router to give more support in situations where you have two levels on the workpieces. The use of masking tape is helpful in the case of sloppy jigs, if you did not get the size quite right; if when you do the test run you discover that your hinge recess is slightly too long, putting some layers of tape on the jig, in the right place, will correct the error.

The use of plastic padding or quick-setting wood filler is also extremely useful, in case of errors in jig making, or if you have managed to take a nick out of the guiding edge of your jig, or damaged it while making it perhaps; such damage can be made good with the filler and the jig reshaped easily.

When making a jig, you must consider how it will be held in position, and also what with – for example G-cramps – so that it will be out of the way of both you and the router while being used.

If the jig is to be used over and over again, and is likely to be subjected to wear, possibly from a pin on a cutter, then it may be necessary to line the edge with, say, plastic laminate. This will stop the edge being slowly worn down; if this is not done, then the more the jig is used, the more out of size it will become. This wear is visible on the edge of the jig in the foreground of fig 117. The jig is edged with white laminate: you can see the white outer layer of the laminate has been worn away by heavy use.

> The use of wax polish on the guiding edges of jigs and fences will help the router to travel smoothly.

Not only are you making the jig to fit your router, but you also need to take into account the size and type of cutter you are going to use: for example, is the bearing at the top or bottom of the cutter? And is your jig going over the workpiece, or under? Try to make your jig simple and strong. When you have finished using the jig, even if it is for a 'one-off' job, it is quite hard to throw it away; it usually gets hung up to collect dust, with the excuse that 'it might get used again one day'!

SHOP-BOUGHT JIGS

The range is increasing all the time. Two major tooling companies that have developed and now sell jigs, are Trend and Titman. The jigs are well made and easy to use, but expensive, unless of course, you are a commercial set-up, in which case they will soon pay for themselves.

USING JIGS

The easiest and simplest way of copying a shape is with the use of a template profiler or trimmer cutter, as these cutters are set with a bearing of the same diameter as the cutter: this means that the bearing runs around the template, and the cutter

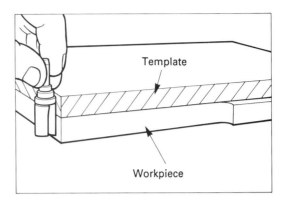

Fig 118 How a template profile cutter works. The template is on top.

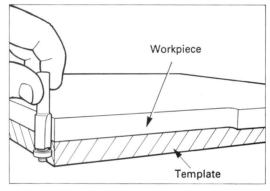

Fig 119 How a trimming cutter works. The template is under the work-piece.

trims back the work-piece to the size and shape of the template. If you can reduce the amount that the cutter has to trim back to the absolute minimum, this will increase the life of the cutter and make the job even easier into the bargain.

In fig 118 you can see the principle of how a template profile cutter works, with the template on the top of the work-piece; fig 119 shows a trimmer cutter working with the template underneath the work-piece. You must remember these cutters are not designed for plunging into the wood: when using them, the router needs to be fixed in plunge mode with the bearing set at the appropriate place on the template. With the use of these cutters you must consider how you are going to keep your template in line with your work-piece: can you screw the template to the work-piece? If not, then can you use G-cramps to hold both together and fixed down on to the bench? (At some point in the process, you may have to reposition the cramps; if one cramp is moved at a time, this can be done without upsetting the alignment of the template.)

Using Guide Bushes for Template and Jig Following

Most of the jigs manufactured by the router tooling companies work on this principle; they use a certain size guide bush, in conjunction with the right size router cutter. The sizes are given with jig specification. As mentioned in Chapter 2, there is a range of different sized guide bushes available.

When making your jig or template, you need to know the size of the cutter you are going to use, and the size of the guide bush. How you come to the size differential between the cutter and bush is up to you, but to show what I mean, look at fig 120. From the edge of the cutter to the outside of the edge of the bush is 4mm on the steel rule, so you must allow this distance when making your jigs. The resulting differential can be seen in fig 121: under the template you can see the 4mm step left once the first cut has been made on the work-piece.

A point to note is that when using a guide bush on corners, as the corner in fig 121 shows (just!), as the guide bush

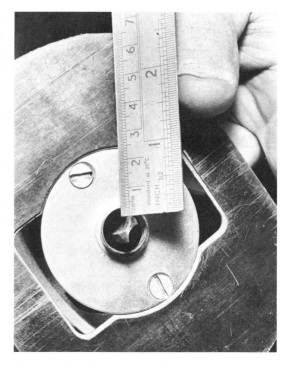

Fig 120 The distance from the edge of the cutter to the outside edge of the guide bush here is 4mm. This will need to be allowed for when making jigs.

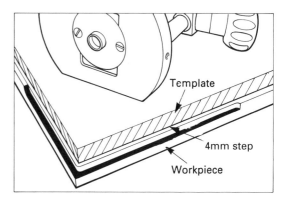

Fig 121 The 4mm step from the template to the edge of the work-piece. You can also see what happens at the corner if you use a guide bush to follow around a square corner: it rounds it off, so is not suitable for this situation.

Fig 122   The underside of the router, with the guide bush in contact with the jig, and the partly trimmed work-piece.

runs around the corner it makes the cutter pivot around, producing a rounded corner, which may not be what is required. Remember this when designing your jig. You may need to use a different method, or a different type of cutter, such as a profile template cutter.

When using guide bushes to guide the router, the cutter used to do the cutting is usually just a standard one with bottom cut, so you are able to plunge the router down into the work-piece and cut down to the full depth in stages, in the normal way, as in fig 123.

You are looking up from under the router and jig, and the router has been stopped at this point to show what is happening. The guide bush is running along the ply template, the first cut has been completed, and part of the next (the cutter is up as if it was on its first cut).

Fig 123   Using the router with a guide bush to follow the shape of the jig.

105

Fig 124   The underside of the jig, showing how the work-piece is held in; the work-piece is on the left.

Guide bushes are most suitable for following curved templates, and the main limitation is size as regards small radius corners: the tighter the inside radius on a corner, the smaller the guide bush needed, and so, also, the smaller the cutter diameter has to be.

Fig 123 shows the same jig being worked the correct way up. The wood to be shaped is held in the jig itself by blocks of wood fixed to the underside of the jig. The work-piece is cut to the exact size to fit in between the blocks. When the jig is cramped in the tail vice, the jig and work-piece are held firm.

Fig 124 shows the battens on the underside of the jig that hold the wood in place in the jig. The partly routed work-piece is also shown.

Butt-Hinge Recessing

A fine example of a useful jig for use with a guide bush, is a jig for butt-hinge recessing, as in fig 125. A piece of wood is held in the vice as a test-piece; the guide bush is fitted to the router and the appropriate cutter. The cutter depth is set to cut to the depth of the hinge plate, below the jig plate thickness. The jig is set in place for the hinge recess to be cut, lined up by means of reference lines; once the jig has been used, of course, there will be the actual cut-out distance cut into the bottom, at the front of the jig, to use to line up with your hinge-line marks. It is a good idea to write on the jig all the details that you will need to set it up for the same process at a later date. The

Fig 125   A hinge jig showing details of cutter and guide bush. Note how it is cramped into place.

details neatly inscribed on the jig in the photo were done especially for the picture; usually they get scribbled on in pencil!

Notice the method of holding the jig in place in fig 125. The front batten not only holds the MDF board square to the work-piece, it is also the method by which the jig is cramped to the work-piece; the batten runs on past the MDF board at each end, making it possible to cramp it to the work-piece easily, and the cramps are also well out of the way of the router, as can be seen in fig 126.

Once routing has taken place, and the jig has been removed, all that remains to be done is to chisel out the back corners by hand and fit the hinge, as in fig 127.

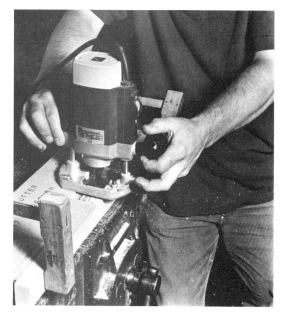

Fig 126   Using the hinge jig.

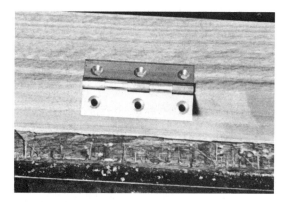

Fig 127   The hinge in the finished recess.

Using Two Jigs

The two jigs in fig 128 were made to be able to rout grooves for inlay lines in the

In some cases it may be necessary to make two jigs to do one job, as shown in fig 128.

back splats of a set of chair backs, as the back splat in the right of the picture shows. The jigs are boards of ⅜in (8mm) MDF with slots 17mm wide cut in them to take a 17mm guide bush. The one on the left has the slots for the straight horizontal lines, and the jig in the centre, the curved vertical lines. The straight slots are easy enough to do by means of working off a straight edge, but the curved ones need a bit more careful setting out with a trammel bar. Getting the ends of

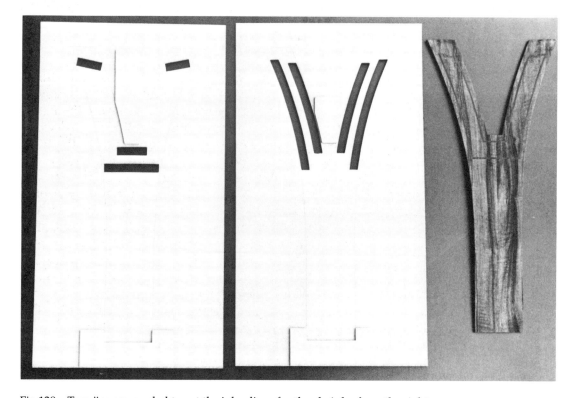

Fig 128   Two jigs are needed to cut the inlay lines for the chair back on the right.

Fig 129   Using the router on a jig made for fluting table legs on a Union Graduate lathe.

the slots right on each jig is especially important as the inlay grooves have to meet at the right place. Also, the basic shape of the splat was crafted with a router and jig; more skill was needed with this job to make the jigs, than to do the work on the splat, each jig relying on the one before being correct and accurate. Apart from that it makes an interesting photograph!

Jigs for Use on a Lathe

The router can be used for fluting, or some other decoration, on turned legs produced on the lathe; to do this you have to make a frame or box that can be mounted on your lathe, to support the router and give it some means of guidance along the turned leg, or whatever. If your lathe has a flat bed, like the Union Graduate, then mounting a box is easy. If your lathe has one or two bars, then a bit more imagination is called for, to work out a way of holding the box to the bars. Once your box is made, you need to be able to hold the leg still, as in fig 129.

I have used a face plate on the outboard end to do this by means of two cramps, one each side of the tool rest, pushed up against the rest and cramped to the face plate. On the face plate are also the reference lines that enable you to space out the fluting equally on the leg: once one cut has been completed, the cramps are released and the face plate is rotated by hand to the next reference line, recramped, and so on.

If you are turning tapered legs of different diameters in reasonable quantity, it may well be worth your while to design and make a box that you can adjust the height of, by means of threaded bars, or by using different sized packer pieces. Only you can decide how much time and effort you want to put into this.

Staircase Jigs

These are easy to use and make, but you must remember that there are complicated building regulations that apply to staircases, so your jigs will have to conform to the correct angle and size of treads and risers. Because of the sizes of the housings needed, the use of a big router is recommended for this job. The cutter used for the staircase housings is usually a low-angled dovetail cutter of about 95 degrees; this will give a sharp edge to the housing, which will then slightly grip into the treads and risers when the wedges are hammered home.

When using a dovetail cutter you must remember to set the cutter to the full depth of cut, as opposed to plunging the cutter, and cut in from the edge of the string (staircase side). Fig 130 shows three different jigs for staircase housings: the top left jig is made for an open-tread staircase with a narrow riser; the top right jig is for a traditional-type staircase with wedge room; and the jig at the bottom of the photo is for a traditional staircase but without wedge room.

The jigs are set at the correct angle by means of battens screwed on to them;

Fig 130   Three different stair housing jigs.

these are transferred from one side of the jig to the other depending on which string of the staircase you are routing. The jigs shown here are home-made out of MDF. Shop-made stair jigs are made by accessory firms, if you wish to buy one ready to use, with a built-in cramping system and a variable-setting guide bar to give the correct angle of the stairs.

7 Cutters

Possibly the best suggestion I can make at this point, is that you go out to your local tool shops, get as many router cutter catalogues as possible, and sit down and read them as if they were a book: the design and manufacture of cutters is a whole science and business in itself.

Try to buy cutters as you need them; this way you will get to know which particular cutter will do what, and also you will find that most cutters will do more than one particular shape or cut. As with most things, you get what you pay for, so the price you can pay is highly variable for what looks like the same cutter, so you need to determine to what and to how much use the cutter will be subjected. But do take into account the fact

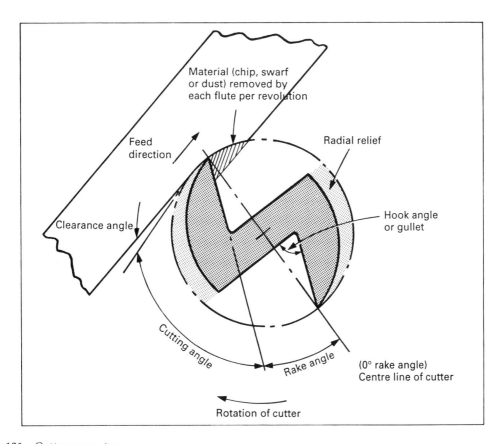

Fig 131   Cutter geometry.

that once you have got the cutter, if you treat it with respect, it will give you great service over and over again.

The average woodworker is mostly interested in what the cutter can do for him, not the intricate details of the main types of metals which are used in the production of the cutters themselves. However, having said that, you do need a basic technical understanding of these to help you select your cutters wisely, and look after them properly.

With the vast range of cutters available, you may think that although your local tool shop only supplies cutters from one manufacturer, he will have the cutter you want, but it is worth bearing in mind that different manufacturers' cutters do vary in size or shape slightly, so keep an open mind if you want a particular cutter for a job. Also, you may want to produce something that can be done with a router only if you could get the right cutter; at this point, it is worth contacting the manufacturers to see if they can make a cutter to suit your needs, and so increase your own production and profit.

When buying cutters, you need to know what shank size your router has: ¼in, ⅜in or ½in imperial, or 6mm, 8mm or 13mm metric. The shank size will in some cases have a great say in what cutters are available to you; this mainly applies to the small routers with ¼in or 6mm collets, as there is a limit to what shape you can make out of a piece of steel and how much force the cutter can be put under. Safety also comes into it, as manufacturers are under a great responsibility to supply safe cutters and tooling.

When you look through the cutter catalogues you must view them with an open mind. The manufacturers give good profile diagrams and sizing, working on the principle that you are working the cutter 90 degrees to the work surface. But remember that your router can work at other angles, either with packers, or by being fixed at an angle, so with a bit of imagination, you can produce shapes and mouldings that are not shown in the catalogues, using standard cutters.

HIGH SPEED STEEL (HSS)

HSS cutters are the cheapest cutters that you can buy, but are not necessarily the most economical. When they are sharp they cut solid timber very cleanly and easily; softwoods and the more easily worked hardwoods are most suited to HSS cutters. One disadvantage is that they need to be kept sharp by regular sharpening, which, if done a lot, will reduce the size of the cutter noticeably; therefore they are not suitable for long production runs. Also, they are easy to damage by overheating: if they are overheated in any way, you never again get a sharp edge on them that will last.

TUNGSTEN CARBIDE

Tungsten Carbide Tips (TCT)

These are cutters that have tungsten carbide brazed on to the cutting edge of the blank cutter, and are then ground to shape. Tungsten carbide is very hard, but brittle: it holds its cutting edge for a long time, and cuts all timber well. This makes it ideal for hard, abrasive woods and man-made boards. It costs more than HSS, but works out to be more economical, because it needs less sharpening time and work devoted to it.

However, tungsten, being very brittle, is also easy to chip if handled carelessly, and only limited home sharpening can be done on tungsten cutters: if they are badly damaged they will need to be sent off to a specialist firm for regrinding, which in turn will mean that they will no longer have their original diameter.

Solid Tungsten Carbide

These are cutters that have been ground to shape from a solid tungsten carbide blank. They basically cut the same materials as TCT but are less prone to failure in some situations where the cutting edge is subject to extreme heat. Care must be taken when using small diameter cutters (less than ¼in/6mm) because, if they are fed too hard and fast, they will break easily.

Replacement, or Disposable Tip Cutters

These are simply steel blanks, to which, by means of very small hexagonal bolts, tungsten blades are attached. These save on 'down' time in production, as, when blunt, the blade can be either taken out and rotated to use another edge, or replaced. In most cases, this can be done without taking the cutter out of the router. Also, if you are in mid-run, the size of the cut will be the same when the blade is refitted. Care must be taken when fitting new blades, to make sure that they are seated properly, and that you don't damage the bolts by over-tightening them.

DIAMOND-TIPPED CUTTERS

As you would imagine, these are the toughest and last the longest, so are usually used for mass production runs.

CUTTER PROFILES

Straight Flute Cutters

Straight flute cutters are the ones most frequently used by the average woodworker. You can get single- or double-fluted cutters. Single-fluted cutters are generally small in diameter. The single flute allows for the back of the cutter to be ground away more, to provide good clearance for the waste wood. This means they will cut relatively fast and with a reasonable finish.

Double-flute cutters give a better finish than single-flute ones, and are also slightly slower as regards feed rate; but do remember that you have two cutting edges, as opposed to one, which also means they last longer. These cutters are best used on hardwoods and man-made boards.

Sheer Flute Cutters

These cutters have the cutting edges angled slightly in the downwards direction, to allow for fast cutting and a good finish, and also to reduce breakout on the top edge when cutting across the grain. In effect, they slice through the wood as opposed to hitting it square on.

Spiral Cutters

As the name suggests, the cutting edges

on these cutters are spiralled, either up or down. Down is suitable for situations such as trimming up veneered and laminated boards; the up cut is suitable for getting wood waste clearance in deep mortise holes and grooves.

Bearing-Guided Cutters

These are cutters fitted with a bearing, either at the top of the cutter or at some point along the cutting edge, usually at the bottom. The bearing is used as a guide for the cutter, either by running along the timber you are cutting, or by running along a template to reproduce that shape. The bearing can be changed for one of a different size, which will alter the profile the cutter will make, making the cutter more versatile.

Provided the bearing is working properly, it should not be marking the timber, or jig.

Pin-Guided Cutters

These work in basically the same way as bearing-guided cutters, except that the pin is fixed and spins at the same speed as the cutter. Because the pin has a relatively small diameter, it is very easy to mark the wood with it. However, being small, the pin does have the advantage of being able to follow tight corners and shapes.

Matching Cutter Sets

These consist of two cutters, where one cutter cuts one half of the joint, and the other cutter the other half. An example of this arrangement is a pair of ovolo joint cutters, which will make a table rule joint, or glazing bar profile and scribe joints.

Dovetail Cutters

A large range of dovetail cutters are available in different sizes and angles. Many of them have been developed to work with particular dovetail jigs; if this is the case, the jig instruction manual will usually tell you which cutters are needed and give reference numbers.

Moulding Cutters

The range is vast, from small oval cutters to large skirting-board mouldings. The smaller moulding cutters can be used in the router free-hand, either running off a bearing or with the router fence fitted. The larger moulding cutters need to be used in fixed machining situations. This is specified in the catalogues.

MAINTENANCE AND SHARPENING OF CUTTERS

Sharpening

The amount of sharpening that can be done by the average woodworker is limited. If the cutter is badly chipped it will need to be ground back to beyond the chip. HSS cutters need aluminium oxide wheels, and TCT cutters need silicon carbide wheels to grind the cutter back. This needs to be done with great care and accuracy, as the same amount needs to be taken off all cutters, and at the same angle. This demands specialist grinders, so the cutter needs to be sent off to a saw doctor, or back to the manufacturer, for sharpening. This may be expensive, so weigh up the cost before you send your cutter away, bearing in mind that depending on how much needs to be ground off, it will certainly alter the size of the cutter; if it is a moulding cutter, this could possibly affect the shape that it will produce next time the cutter is used. If a lot of steel has been removed from the cutter face, then the clearance angle may have been affected, which in turn will mean that the back of the cutting edge may also need to be reshaped, to produce the original clearance angle. If the clearance angle is not kept, the performance of the cutter will be reduced.

If the cutter is only blunt, and not damaged, you can restore it to a keen, sharp edge by hand sharpening. This can be done with ordinary sharpening stones; some, however, are better suited to the job than others. The standard oil stone, India and Carborundum, will sharpen HSS cutters, but very slowly. Japanese water stones are more effective and faster on HSS but the stones are easily worn down, so great care must be taken to keep them flat, which is not easy if you are using them to sharpen a lot of cutters.

Diamond whetstones are a great invention for home sharpening: not only will they sharpen HSS, but also tungsten carbide. These diamond whetstones are constructed with a colour-coded base made from glass-fibre reinforced polycarbonate; the plastic is then injection moulded with a precision-perforated steel plate. Finally monocrystalline diamonds are partially embedded into nickel, which is electroplated on to a steel face.

These sharpening stones come in a variety of sizes, grits and shapes; they are quite expensive, but well worth the money considering what you can use them for. You use a small amount of water with them to lubricate them and to wash away the steel particles when in use. Being diamond, they work fast and easily, even on tungsten carbide; in my opinion, this is the only sharpening tool worth trying to sharpen tungsten carbide with.

When sharpening, or honing, a cutter with a hand stone, it is important to keep the front face of the cutter flat on the

Fig 132   Sharpening a cutter on a DMT sharpening stone.

stone; try to make the same number of strokes along the stone on each blade, for if the cutter is only dull or blunt, it will not take many strokes to restore its sharpness. On HSS you may find that you can get a burr on the cutting edge. This needs to be taken off gently with the sharpening stone following the shape of the cutter.

With bearing-guided cutters, you need to remove the bearing before sharpening. At this point it may also be worth cleaning off any resin that has built up, using a solvent. This will also help prevent your sharpening stone becoming clogged up.

Cleaning and Lubricating

After you have sharpened your cutter, it is worth spraying it with either a light oil, PTFE spray, which is a dry lubricant, or a silicon spray. The last two are very good at slowing down the build-up of resin on the cutter. The use of a spray lubricant prolongs the life expectancy of cutters very effectively by stopping rust if your workshop is damp, as well as keeping the cutters clean.

Bearings have to be cleaned with as little solvent as possible, as the bearings are sealed for life; if the grease does dissolve, then the bearing is likely to be at the end of its life. The bearings are considered to be expendable items, but on the odd occasion where a bearing has become partially seized during a run, I have managed to get it working by dropping it into some oil to get it to run freely again. I know this is not recommended, but it does get the job completed.

Laminate trimming is extremely hard on bearings, because the adhesive builds up around the bearing and especially between the bearing and the cutter. The best way, I find, to deal with this is to pick the glue off with a small knife and spray often with a lubricant to prevent it sticking on too hard. The pins of pin cutters need to be cleaned at regular intervals, for if resin builds up on the pin it soon starts to burn, leaving a scorch mark on the wood.

Suspect Cutters

If you think that you have purchased a cutter that is faulty, return it! I am glad to say this is now a rare event. Faults to look out for are gaps on the jointing of tungsten-tipped cutters, pins on pin cutters not being true, or, if a pin cutter has been reground, the pin having also been cut into by the grinding wheel – this will reduce the contact area of the pin and possibly cut into the wood as it is being used.

If a cutter has been reground many times, the amount of steel left will become smaller and smaller, and this will mean that the cutter itself will become vulnerable to breakage; at some point you will need to make the decision to throw it out before the router throws it out at you!

The shanks of cutters must not be pitted or scored in any way, because this may damage the collet on the router, or even worse, the cutter may come out.

Storing of Cutters

When new, they come in plastic cases, with the cutter enclosed in protective wax, which you remove before use. The plastic cases are fine when the cutters are covered in wax, but once the wax is removed the cutter soon cuts its way through the case; so one of the best ways

Fig 133   Cutters stored in a block.

of keeping your cutters is in a block of wood with holes drilled to the shank size of the cutters. The cutters are then stored sticking safely upwards, and are easily visible when you want to pick out the cutter you want to use; mounting cutters together in this way also makes it easy and quick to spray them with lubricant every now and then. The careful storage of cutters is worthwhile, as they soon add up to a lot of money, if you constantly have to repair or replace them.

8 Site Use of Routers

For the purpose of this book, I will define site use as any work done outside the workshop. This can be on large building sites where the whole building is under construction, or for alterations and improvements in the domestic home.

The important point about working on building sites, and one which is coming into force more and more, is the compulsory use of 110-volt tools. 110 volts won't kill you, whereas 240 volts may. For routers, this is no big deal, as most manufacturers make 110-volt routers already. They look the same, and behave the same as 240-volt ones, but with a very slight loss of power, in most cases not enough to notice. For most site work, a large, heavy-duty router is required.

What you will notice with your 110-volt router, is that when using it off a normal 240-volt supply, you will have to hump around a transformer, which weighs 40lb (18kg). For safety reasons 110-volt machines are fitted with round three-pin plugs, which can only be used with 110-volt supply sockets.

SITE-WORK APPLICATIONS

Cutting

What site work you are doing, and what other site machines you have, will determine to what use you put your router. It may just be used to cut up sheet materials, such as ply, chipboard MDF or plastic laminate, to size. The advantages of using a router are that you don't have to manhandle an 8 × 4ft (2.4 × 1.2m) sheet over a site saw, which in most cases is not very easy, especially if you are on your own, or limited to the width of cut that the fence of the saw can be set to. Using a hand-saw may get over the problem, but even if you are extremely skilled with one, it will leave a rough edge. On the other hand, with the router and a suitable cutter, a straight edge (such as a board and two G-cramps), and the ply, or whatever, supported either on trestles or off the floor with battens, you can cut up the board to the size required, and produce a clean edge. Just clamp the straight edge on to the board, allowing for the distance from the cutter to the edge of the router base, which will run along the straight edge.

Form-Work

Don't forget that a trammel bar can produce perfect semi-circles for form work on arch-topped doors and windows.

Edge Planing

The router used as an edge planer on site is extremely useful. Again, with just a straight edge, doors and panels can be trimmed to size, and the edge will be at 90 degrees to the face of the door and clean. The availability of a straight cutter with a cutting depth of 2½in (60mm) means that all standard doors are easily dealt with in this way. The router can be used to cut access holes and panels in floors and wall panels. You may be able to re-use the section that you have cut out, buying the additional battens to form a hatch, or you may wish to cut a hole for a purpose-made cover.

Access Holes

Trend supply a jig and fitting designed for access holes, called the Routabout (*see* fig 134). It consists of a template that is screwed to the floor where the access hole is required, the screw being the pivot point of the template. The router is attached to the template with a 30mm guide bush, and is fitted with a special cutter that cuts a rebated groove as the router is rotated around the pivot. A purpose-made ring is supplied, which fits into the rebated hole once the middle section has been removed. The template is unscrewed from the middle section, which is then turned over and re-used to fill the access hole.

Mouldings

The use of a router to put mouldings on architraves and skirting boards is sometimes a viable proposition on site, depending on the shape of the moulding. You may be able to use the router hand-

Fig 134   The Routabout by Trend.

held, or it may have to be set up in a table.

Flooring

In some cases you may find when fitting a floor, that to finish it off, you will need to cut up boards to make in-fills, for example for thresholds in doorways, or for odd corners. The tongues and grooves can be made either with straight cutters, with two or three set-ups, or with one pass with a special tongue-and-groove cutter that matches the tongue and grooves of the floor-boards.

Window-Boards

Window-boards are sometimes delivered on site just as prepared timber, without the tongue on the board to fit into the groove in the inside of the window-sill, or without a bull-nose on the front edge of the board. This may be because no sizes were given to the supplier, or because the window reveal is such an odd shape that it is just supplied over-size, to be fitted on site. The tongue can be formed using a straight cutter and fence, or a rebate cutter with a bearing, working from the underside of the board. The bull-nose can be formed with the use of an ovolo, or rounding-over cutter with a router fence, or a bearing-guided ovolo cutter with the bigger bearing fitted.

Door Furniture

With hinges, depending on how many there are to be cut, and whether they are the same size throughout the job, you may decide it is worthwhile using a jig to guide the router, and getting a mini production line going to cut the hinge recesses on the doors. Or you may decide to mark out the hinge recess in the normal way, and use the router free-hand as a bulk waste remover, giving you a nice, level bottom hinge recess, and leaving only a small amount of hand chiselling-out to do, cutting back to your lines. The hinge recesses on the door styles may need more thought, as you may not be able to use the jig used on the door itself because the door-stops may already have been fitted. With a slight modification to your jig, namely a packer to take up the thickness of the door-stop, and by increasing the depth setting of the router, you will get over this small problem.

Mortise Locks

A heavy duty router is best suited to the cutting out of mortise lock housings, because of the depth at which they are housed in the edge of the door, usually 2–2½in (50–60mm). If the router is set up as for cutting a mortise hole, with two fences, this will make the operation a lot easier; furthermore you won't get any problems with the lock not being set into the door squarely. The mortise lock cover plate is quite often tricky to fit, because of the very shallow recess required, and, with thin doors, you quite often have to work very near the edge. If someone is a bit heavy-handed with a chisel, it can go right through the corner, making a mess of the recess, whereas the router is very suitable for cutting a shallow recess close to edges.

There are, of course, commercially made jigs for fitting mortise locks, but you need to weigh up the cost of these against how much you would use them. You may find that by investing in a second fence and the right cutters, you can improve your production and quality using an ordinary router.

Letter-Box Holes

Cutting a letter box is a very suitable job for the router. You can either use a straight edge to run the router against, or, if you fit a lot of letter boxes, it may be worth purchasing a purpose-made jig, such as the Trend letter-box jig (*see* fig 135). Made from cast aluminium, the jig is adjustable to enable cut-outs to be made from 210 × 46mm to 310 × 82mm (8¼ × 1¾in to 12¼ × 3¼in).

Weather Strips

These are permanent door and window seals, rather than temporary stick-on weather seals. It is quite an easy job to fit a good-quality rubber seal, as well as a brush draught excluder to the underside edge of a door. These are held in place by a narrow groove usually ⅛in (2–3mm) wide, and ¼in (6mm) deep. It is an ideal job for a router with a slotting or a groover cutter fitted on to the appropriate arbor, which gives you, in effect, a miniature saw blade. The depth of the cut is set by the use of the correct size bearing on the arbor, in relation to the slotter diameter.

The use of industrial weather stripping could previously only be done effectively when the doors and windows were being made in the factory; now, by using a router with an appropriate slotter, any individual can improve the draught proofing in his home.

Old Doors and Windows

In many instances, the router can be used to rout out rotten timber, giving a clean

Fig 135 The letter-box hole template by Trend.

smooth hole or rebate, into which new timber can be fixed. This applies mainly to doors and window openers, which can be unhinged and worked on flat, preferably at ground level!

Work-Tops

The router with a groove cutter fitted is also useful for making grooves in work-tops which are then going to be fitted with solid wood edging strips. A groove can be made in the work-top, and the same groove run in the edging strips; then a loose tongue can be cut to size and fitted into the two grooves. By using, say, a ¼in (6mm) slotter and a strip of ¼in (6mm) ply, you will be able to perfectly align the pieces to be joined, and increase the gluing area.

121

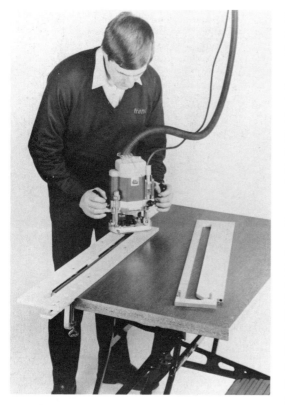

Fig 136   Postform (work-top) jig.

The jointing of work-tops, especially where two tops need to be joined at right angles to one another, is a problem if the front edges are preformed to a shape. This needs then to be mitred at the moulded section, which can be done with the careful use of straight edges, or by using a ready-made jig. Two companies that produce jigs to perform the jointing of work-tops are Titman and Trend. Made from aluminium or Tufnol, there are several variations available for fitting together work-tops, for cutting up to 39in (1m) wide and 1½in (40mm) thick. Incorporated in these jigs, or as a separate jig, are panel-butt connector jigs. These are used together with the recom-

mended cutter and guide bush. These jigs need to be used with the heavy-duty routers needed for most site work.

The router can also be used to produce cut-outs in work-tops for cooker hobs, washing-up bowls or sinks, by using the router against straight edges or with a guide bush and appropriate jig, if many of the same size cut-outs are required. If fitting a round sink bowl, use the router with a trammel bar.

Office Desks

Another useful purpose a router can be put to is the alteration of desk-tops, necessary because of the ever-advancing technology in offices. Computers, and their peripheral technology, are constantly updated, and, in a lot of cases, new models are different sizes from the originals for which the desks were designed; rather than buy new desks, it is quite often possible with a router and some clever cramping of a straight edge, to alter the recess in order to accommodate the new technology.

When carrying out alterations to already occupied sites, such as offices, you will need to consider how to protect the area around where you are working from the dust produced by a router. The use of a domestic vacuum cleaner may improve the situation: get someone to hold the nozzle in the line of fire of the dust coming from the cutter.

Plastic Laminates

These can be trimmed up very successfully by the router with a suitable cutter, on site or back at the workshop. I know it is not easy to do, but the smaller the amount of laminate to be trimmed, the

Fig 137   Office alterations of desk tops. Note the transformer, just in the picture on the right, and the protective covering against dust behind the operator.

better it will be for the life expectancy of the cutter. You must use tungsten cutters for this.

Drilling

This is an underrated use of the router, the big advantage being that you always get a hole cut at 90 degrees to the face surface. With the use of counter-bore and plug cutters, screws can be hidden away very tidily in site situations.

Sharp Edges

For a better finished appearance, or to

123

reduce the chance of personal injury on protrusions, the use of a router with either a rounding-over or a chamfer cutter, will remedy sharp edges safe, quickly and accurately.

TOOL USE ON SITE

One of the problems with site work, including humping the tools in and out of the vehicle, is that it is extremely tough on tools and tooling. As the router and its cutters are quite easily damaged, and because there is nothing more frustrating than spending five long minutes looking for a spanner to change cutters, when it should take only seconds, it is worth spending a bit of time making a strong box, with some method of storing the cutters safely, to keep all your bits and pieces together.

Once you begin to use a router on site, and come across situations where you think you can use the router, you wonder why you haven't thought of it before! And then the more you use the router, the more cutters you collect, and this in turn opens up more possibilities for its use.

Glossary

Arbor A metal shaft on to which different groovers, slotters and bearings can be fitted.

Back cutting Running the router (cutter) in the opposite direction to the normal direction of feed. The router is being fed in the same direction as the cutter is spinning.

Band saw A machine that drives a continuous, narrow blade to cut wood on, often used to cut curves.

Batten A piece of timber of relatively small section – about 2 × 1in (50 × 25mm).

Bead Small, semi-circular moulding. If the bead is above the surface, it is called a cocked bead; if below the surface, a sunk bead.

Breakout Where the wood has splintered out when machined; this happens more often when working across the grain.

Burr A small cutter with lots of cutting edges, usually spiralling around the shape of the cutter. It is used in a machine free-hand for carving and cleaning up.

Chamfer An angled edge, machined or planed on to the wood, to take away a 90-degree corner.

Chipboard Man-made board, made with wood particles and resin.

Collet Another name for a chuck, used to grip and hold cutters in a machine.

Collet nut A hexagonal nut used to hold the collet in the router spindle.

Concave The inside of a curve or hollowed-out shape.

Convex The outside of a curve shape.

Cove Usually a quarter circle used as a decoration, or part of a moulding.

Cramping (or clamping) Pulling together two or more pieces, to hold them tight (to immobilize them while machining or gluing).

Depth stop Device used to set the required depth to be cut.

Dovetail A two-part joint, one part of which is cut to the shape of a dove's tail, while the second (the pin) is cut to receive the shape of the dovetail. This is often used in drawer and box jointing.

Dowel Either a round wooden peg, or a flat, oval piece of wood (also called a 'biscuit'), which forms a mechanical joint between two pieces of timber.

End vice (or tail vice) This is fitted at one end of a work-bench, and usually holds work steady on the bench while it is being worked on, by means of a *dog* – a small piece of metal that can be raised or lowered with the bench surface.

Fence A guide surface for the machine that runs along the work-piece, or against which the work-piece is pushed. It is usually a straight edge at 90 degrees to the machine base or table.

Flute The cut away part of a cutter that leads to the cutting edge.

Form work (or shuttering) This is used on building sites, to form temporary structures to support brickwork or concrete.

G-cramp Cramp in the shape of a G.

Grain The texture of the wood. The grain direction of a board is the direction of growth of a tree. End grain is a cross-section of a tree.

Guide bush A round metal bush with a flat flange for fixing to a router. It is used to guide the router on a defined path.

High-speed steel A metal alloy used by manufacturers to produce cutters that will hold a cutting edge well, as well as being capable of taking the heat and strains that the cutter will be subjected to when used.

Housing   Usually a trench made across a board of wood to receive another board at an angle to the first, to form a joint between the two.

Jig   An object that holds the work-pieces and guides the tools operating on or in them.

MDF (medium density fibreboard)   A man-made board material made from reconstructed wood and resin.

Mitre   The bisected line of the joint of two pieces of wood, used, for example, in picture frames.

Moisture meter   A device that measures the percentage of moisture present in timber.

Mortise and tenon   A joint used in wood-work. The mortise is a square or rectangular hole cut into one piece of wood, and the tenon is formed as a tongue on the end of a rail, which goes into the mortise hole.

Moulding   A form of decoration made on or in the surface of wood.

Ovolo   A type of moulding with a convex quarter-round shape, the top and bottom of the round are stepped.

Parallel bars   Two bars set apart at an equal distance, used to guide the router by the width between the bars or by means of a guide bush.

Pin cutter   A cutter that has a round piece at the bottom of it that runs along the wood as a guide. The pin is part of the cutter, and cannot be removed; whereas a bearing-guided cutter has a bearing instead of the pin and this rotates freely.

Pivot point   A fixed point that something rotates around.

Ply   A man-made board, made up of thin layers of wood, layered in opposite directions and held together with resin.

Pressure pad   A pad that is used to put pressure on the work-piece to keep it against the fence or table.

PTFE spray (poly-tetra-fluoro-ethylene spray)   A dry lubricant, ideal for use on router shafts to keep them running smoothly.

Push stick   A piece of wood used to push work-pieces past the cutter, rather than using your fingers, just in case you slip!

Quick-release cramp   A cramp that will adjust in size quickly, with only a minimum of screw-turning to tighten up; or it will tighten by means of a cam-lever.

Rebate   Also referred to as *rabbit*, this is a rectangular cut-out along an edge of a piece of work.

Spline   A piece of material used to join two pieces together by being inserted into a groove in each piece.

Template   A shape used as a guide to reproduce another identical shape.

Test-pieces   These are off-cuts that are used to check your router settings before you cut into the real work-piece.

Trammel bar   A long arm, one end of which has a pivot point, while the other end is attached to a device for marking or cutting arcs and circles.

Tungsten carbide   A very hard but brittle metal used for cutters; it can be used just for tips, or for whole cutters.

Turret Stop   A depth stop device that has more than one height setting.

Water stone   This is a sharpening stone that uses water as a lubricant, as opposed to an oil stone which uses oil.

Weather strip   A rubber gasket used as a draught-proofer in windows and doors.

Wood-packer   Off-cut used when cramping, so that the workpiece is not damaged with cramp pressure marks. It is also used to pack up pieces when necessary.

Index